Praise for thi

"Juliana is a very experienced Escrow Officer. Her years of experience with diverse and difficult transactions show through in this very informative, yet entertaining book. This is a subject that all who invest or work in real estate should know about but very few do— "Escrow, just what is it?" She very cleverly answers that question. I commend Juliana for taking the initiative to help buyers and sellers better understand how their transaction progresses through a lot of twists and turns to completion."

—Beulah Stidham, President, Madrona Park Escrow, Inc.
2012 President of Escrow Institute of California

"The Art of Escrow is a must have for anyone considering buying or selling property in California. This is a witty, elegant and passionate book—educational and entertaining. Ms.Tu brings her passion for her profession to life."

—Donna Inman, CSEO, CEI
2013 President, California Escrow Association

"The Art of Escrow is an excellent step-by-step guide to take both the new home buyer or seller and the real estate practitioner through the escrow process. If you are buying a home, selling a home, or acting as an agent, this guide will provide an easy understanding to this often complex and sometimes stressful experience. As we say in the business, 'a house will sell itself, it takes a professional to guide you through the process,' and I cannot think of a better guide than The Art of Escrow by certified escrow officer Juliana Tu. Juliana served as my escrow consultant for my best selling text, California Real Estate Principles, now in its 8th edition."

—Charles "Buck" Stapleton, GRI
Professor, West Los Angeles College
Co-author of California Real Estate Principles
Master Instructor, California Association of REALTORS®

"I have been in the escrow business for over 48 years. I really appreciate how well Juliana has mapped out the course of the escrow process and helped identify the scenery and the intricacies of the many stops along the way. This book is an easy read, very educational and is packed full of practical tools for understanding the entire escrow route. Juliana offers real and sensible insights and tips for anyone involved in the process of acquiring property. I recommend this reading for anyone reaching out for the 'American Dream.'"

—David A. Shean, CSEO/CEI/CNSA
Principal, Escrow Essentials & First Class Signing Services
1988 President of the California Escrow Association and long time active member of the American Escrow Association

"Anyone considering purchasing or selling a house would be well advised to invest in this very clearly written guide to avoiding all the risks and pitfalls of such an expensive venture, which at first sight seems incredibly complicated. Like a natural-born teacher, the author takes you by little steps through the entire process, not only painlessly, but interestingly—even for a reader not involved in buying or selling a piece of real estate. Her writing style will keep you turning the pages, which are cleverly illustrated."

—**John Dombrowski**, MA, MLS; Writer, Editor & Historian

"Whenever there is an extremely difficult escrow challenge, such as succession of an estate, Juliana Tu is the go-to person. I know that the transaction will be handled expeditiously and legally. The Art of Escrow would be a great guide for the beginner who is purchasing their first home, or a seasoned real estate professional. There is always something to learn from Juliana."

—**Esther S.M. Chao**, General Partner, Giant Panda Management
Producer of "American Fusion", the movie
Author of *Red, White and Blue in the U.S.A.*

The Art *of* Escrow

The Art *of* Escrow

The Fight For Your American Dream

and the Pursuit of Homeownership

Juliana Tu, CSEO, CEO, CBSS, CEI

Published by Advantage, Charleston, South Carolina.
Member of Advantage Media Group.

ADVANTAGE is a registered trademark and the Advantage colophon is a trademark of Advantage Media Group, Inc.

Printed in the United States of America.

ISBN: 978-159932-353-4
LCCN: 2012954108

This publication is designed to provide accurate and authoritative information in regard to the subject matter covered. It is sold with the understanding that the publisher is not engaged in rendering legal, accounting, or other professional services. If legal advice or other expert assistance is required, the services of a competent professional person should be sought.

 Advantage Media Group is proud to be a part of the Tree Neutral® program. Tree Neutral offsets the number of trees consumed in the production and printing of this book by taking proactive steps such as planting trees in direct proportion to the number of trees used to print books. To learn more about Tree Neutral, please visit www.treeneutral.com. To learn more about Advantage's commitment to being a responsible steward of the environment, please visit www.advantagefamily.com/green

Advantage Media Group is a leading publisher of business, motivation, and self-help authors. Do you have a manuscript or book idea that you would like to have considered for publication? Please visit www.advantagefamily.com or call 1.866.775.1696

This book is dedicated to all of my fellow overworked and underappreciated escrow professionals. Never forget that you are the glue that holds the transaction together. It is your knowledge and expertise that allows your clients to sell or buy with peace of mind. This book is written in celebration of the importance of what you do and with the hope that with better understanding of the process, your clients will give you the acknowledgment and appreciation that you deserve.

Acknowledgements

I want to thank my family. My husband, Kenneth I. Ma, my son Trevor, and my daughter Justine, who pushed me, encouraged me, supported me and would not take "no" for an answer. Without them, these words would never have made it on to this paper.

To my assistants, Rebecca Barasorda and Teresa Dang, my appreciation knows no bounds. It was your help handling my workload that gave me the time and peace of mind that I needed to put this book together.

I also want to thank the very talented Amanda Loka, whose illustrations give life and depth throughout the book.

Table of Contents

CHAPTER ONE: Why This Book?   17

What Mr. Wyznovski Taught Me

I Have Come a Long Way, Baby

That "Ah, Ha!" Moment

No One Likes to Be Misunderstood

CHAPTER TWO: First, It's Back to the Basics   31

Abiding by a Certain Code

It's All about Trust

And to Provide an Accounting

And Then There Are Those Other Important Reasons. . .

We Are Not All Alike

It's Not Just Homes

Relationships Matter

Location, Location, Location

CHAPTER THREE: Before We Get to the Table   63

Your Greatest Strength: Preparation

The Seller: "I Am Going to Ask for the World"

Whereas, for the Buyer: "How Low Can I Go?"

**CHAPTER FOUR: What Can I Expect in
a Transaction?**   75

Time for the Nitty-Gritty

Just How Do We Spend Our Time?

Money Makes the World Go Round

The "Oh-No!" Section, or Why It Can Sometimes Become a Fight

CHAPTER FIVE: The Actual Process 101

Juggling

The Strange Concept of Title Insurance

Buyer's Responsibilities, Part One: Doing Due Diligence

Buyer's Responsibilities, Part Two: Getting That Loan

Seller's/Borrower's Responsibilities

Your Escrow Is Closed! or The Battle is Won!

CHAPTER SIX: Other Types of Transactions 133

Your Home, Your Castle, Your Bank: Refinance Transactions

Underwater and Sinking Fast: Short Sale Transactions

Sunk! or Losing the Fight: The REO Transaction

CHAPTER SEVEN: In Conclusion 149

The Professional

APPENDICES 155

Appendix A: Escrow, in the Center of Things

Appendix B: Life of an Escrow (Timeline)

Appendix C: How the Cash Flows

Appendix D: Vestings: How to Take Title to a Property (California Style)

Appendix D-2: Vestings for Individual Ownership

Appendix E: The Crazy Language of Escrow

Disclaimer

Although the stories used as examples in this book are based on real events, the names have been changed to protect the confidentiality of my customers.

The information and ideas contained in this book are intended to provide insight and understanding, not advice, concerning real estate transactions and the escrow process. The reader is cautioned to seek his own legal and financial counsel for his particular transaction. No representations by the author are made and the information provided herein is intended only as a guide.

As laws change from year to year and as escrow processing information, as delineated in this book, are subject to local customs and/or regional/government requirements, the reader is instructed to check with their escrow professional for up-to-date changes in laws and regulations that may affect his transaction.

1

Why This Book?

CHAPTER ONE

Why This Book?

WHAT MR. WYZNOVSKI TAUGHT ME

I am starting my story with a certain Mr. Stefan Wyznovski, an elderly man of about seventy years of age when I first met him. He had an eight-unit apartment building that he was selling and, having come from a background in which a "man's handshake" was as good as gold, he was absolutely confounded by the whole process of selling his property. When I handed him the paperwork he needed to complete, he almost balked and walked out. In fact, the only reason he was in my office that day was to take a look at the person who was supposed to help him sell the piece of real estate he had owned for more than thirty years. He was a "gentleman of the old school" and probably looked askance at the abilities of this Chinese woman half his age.

The transaction took more than sixty days to complete and Mr. Wyznovski must have called me almost every single day to find out why he needed to provide the information I requested, where we were, and what was going to happen next. Needless to say, when I was able to successfully close his escrow and hand him his check, I breathed a huge sigh of relief, feeling as if I had accomplished an absolute miracle. This glow of success stayed with me for weeks. As

I was to find out over the years, that feeling comes every time we do a good job for our customer, whether it is a marathon transaction or a sprint.

Mr. Wyznovski's case helped me realize the importance of consumers understanding the escrow process. Without this understanding, they feel a lack of control. They get nervous and try to micromanage their case, calling constantly for updates. Other times they are hesitant to provide information when, in fact, providing it would actually help them. When customers know what is happening, what is expected of them, and what they can expect from us, the process becomes less stressful, more productive, and more enjoyable for all parties involved.

With Mr. Wyznovski, I realized that this practice of "escrow," as it is called in California (it is known as "settlement services" or "closing services" throughout the rest of the nation), is an important but misunderstood part of the whole process, the process of achieving the American dream and owning a home. In this land of immigrants, achieving this American dream means You Have Made It.

The escrow process is not difficult to understand, but ask any consumer out there, and I promise you nine out of ten won't know what it involves. Everyone knows they are supposed to do something

in order to achieve the end result, but what must be done and how it is all pulled together within a designated time period is a total mystery. What I want to do in this book is demystify the process.

I HAVE COME A LONG WAY, BABY

Have you ever heard the slogan, "You've come a long way, baby"? I am probably dating myself, but when I was studying for my degree at Sweet Briar College, Virginia, this was the advertising slogan put out by the Virginia Slims cigarette brand. Yes, remember that? The company's slogan and advertisement campaign told people that women were starting to step out of the traditional roles assigned to them. Here we were, up-and-coming women, stepping out of our stereotypical boxes. This slogan had extra meaning for me because I was an immigrant back in the 1970s, and I have come a long, long way.

Like almost all of the old timers in this industry, I fell into the escrow profession by chance. There was never a decision in college that I was going to be an escrow officer—not like, "I am going to be an attorney, or a doctor, or a teacher." I didn't even know there was such a thing as "escrow" back then.

In 1977, when I started work at a local bank, I was young, impressionable, and full of energy. Banks were the settlement service providers at that time, and I guess the qualities I exhibited were important because before I knew it, I was assigned to a certain department and, like Alice in Wonderland, dropped into this strange world of "escrow." Mad Hatter? Check. Cheshire Cat? Double check. The Escrow Queen? Oh, absolutely!

But once in it, I found I had a knack for it. I enjoyed the problem-solving part, and the detailed organization aspect of it, I guess because I am a perfectionist and a bit of a control freak.

I also liked the person-to-person contact with my clients. I didn't even mind the tons of paperwork involved.

I found out later that a good 90 percent of the people working in escrow simply fell into it, just as I had. But that has changed in the last ten years. Children of the old timers followed their parents into the business, knowing in advance what they were getting into. Real estate professionals are also more aware of escrow as a career because it is an affiliated industry. Their children are also entering the profession.

But back then it was a bit of a lonely thing, as there were not that many of us around and it was hard to find a mentor who could help me along. This was not an industry that was known or well organized at the time. But as in most life-changing situations, there is a defining moment, and for me it came when I realized that there was a professional organization with monthly educational meetings to teach me what I did not know. All of a sudden I realized there was a small world of people just like me, who had the same problems I had, the same questions, and the same goals. All of a sudden I had many mentors I could call on, and they all belonged to the California Escrow Association.

You probably wonder what makes me the right person to write this book. It's not just the fact that throughout the years many of my friends and peers have encouraged me to do so, but also because thirty-five years in any one industry will give any person considerable knowledge and experience. In thirty-five years you will come across all sorts of strange and intricate problems that make for good stories. Remember, it's not just the home we live in with our treasured family memories that we handle escrows on. There are sales of other types of properties, including commercial properties, new subdivisions, and condominiums. There are loan transactions for not only single families but also commercial and construction loan transactions. There are also sales of businesses, with or without land—hotels/motels, gas stations, laundromats, restaurants—and now, REO properties and short sale transactions, which really are all in a class of their own.

I am going to own up to the fact that I love giving seminars. Seminars are a popular forum for teaching, and I love teaching and found that I was not afraid of the podium. When I joined the Escrow Association, I was called on to educate my peers through seminars. That progressed into educating not only people in my profession but also those in the real estate profession—the real estate companies and their up-and-coming agents. I gave seminars to government agencies, including, believe it or not, the Internal Revenue Service. Even IRS agents were interested in finding out about our process. Finally, I did a stint teaching escrow at Pasadena City College in my area.

Over the last few years I have been writing a monthly newsletter that is emailed to my clients. I use this as an opportunity to educate my clients on the escrow process and bring them up to date with news and events of interest.

So with all this writing and teaching, can a book tie it all together?

There is a difference between book knowledge and on-the-job experience. To excel in anything, you have to have a combination of both, probably more of the latter than the former. There certainly are books written on the processing of an escrow that an entry-level person can study. But you can study all you want; nothing beats working at an actual job, especially when you work through and survive the highs and the lows of the real estate industry.

What has happened in the last thirty-five years?

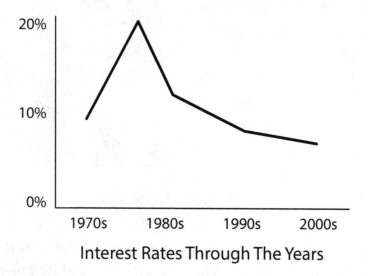

Interest Rates Through The Years

Remember the early 1980s when interest rates on mortgages shot to astronomical levels of 19 and 20 percent? I learned all about "creative financing"—the bypassing of traditional methods of obtaining a loan—during those days. This was the period of all-inclusive trust deeds, seller carry-back loans, "subject-to" purchases, and land contracts. Today's new generation of escrow officers may rarely hear and never handle one of these types of transactions, but I cut my eye teeth on them. Rates may have been high those years, but property values were still very affordable, so with a little creative financing the market was still going strong.

Then came the late 1980s when the high mortgage rates dropped, creating a boom in real estate sales. Properties flipped, once, twice, sometimes even three times a year. Those were also the years during which a lot of Japanese conglomerates snapped up American real estate left and right and invested in high-rises and multimillion dollar projects. Remember that?

The boom didn't last, and by the early 1990s, property values capped out. It was time for the downward slide again. What goes up must come down, and vice versa. We all know what happened in the early 2000s. Money became easy to obtain again and it was the start of the refinance craze. The saying in our industry was, "if you were breathing, you could get a loan." Property values reached stratospherical levels and instead of the Japanese conglomerates, we saw the start of foreign investments by Chinese individuals.

I have to admit that I barely remember the years between 2003 through 2007. It all passed in such a blur. What I can remember makes me shudder. It was work, work, work, sometimes until midnight and always on the weekends. Did we coin "24/7" during those heydays?

I saw hundreds of refinance transactions pass across my desk, and almost all of the loans obtained were adjustable-rate loans, which means the rates and monthly payments would jump dramatically, sometimes just in a few short months. My clients would sit at my desk signing documents, and I wondered if they even cared that their payments were going to make a huge jump in six short months. I distinctly remember one particular lady talking with her sister about all of the name-brand purses and shoes she was buying, this while signing her life away. It was all about luxury items and these luxury items were being paid for through her refinance. In other words, her house was a piggybank. Every time she needed something new, she got an appraisal, which showed that her property had jumped up in value, and she would be back at the signing table again.

Were consumers using the money they took out of their home each time to make more money? Most of them, I think, were spending it on luxury items: vacation homes, trips, and things like that. When the real estate bubble burst, these people were left with nothing but a house that was going to be "under water," or worth less than what was owed on it. The writing was on the wall and it looked grim.

In 2007, I was interviewed by the *Los Angeles Times* about the state of our real estate and escrow industry and that writing on the wall. The article was titled "Mortgage Meltdown," and although others might have felt that I sounded too pessimistic at the time, I guess the years after that unfortunately proved me right on the money. The "mortgage meltdown" turned into a depressing "how low can it go"?

So, in answer to the question, "why are you qualified to write this book Juliana?", the qualification comes from thirty-five years' worth of accumulated knowledge and on-the-job experience—thirty-five years of riding the market through its highs and its lows, thirty-five years of stories to tell!

It is my honor and duty to "pay it forward" to my clients, to the real estate professionals, the general public, and especially to the next generation of escrow officers. Knowledge and experience counts for nothing if it is not used to benefit others and the upcoming generation.

So, to all my friends who have encouraged me and pushed me through the years, I am finally writing this book. I have come a long way, baby.

THAT "AH HA!" MOMENT

Thirty-five years later, after any number of Mr. Wyznovskis, I am not so young. I am less impressionable, and my energy has waned just a little bit. But the enthusiasm I have for this profession remains strong. What have I learned these past years? I have learned that no one outside my industry really knows what we do. It's like a secret that we keep for ourselves, a mystery! But mysteries are not good because by not teaching people what we do and, more importantly, why we do things a certain way, we are doing the Mr. Wyznovskis and ourselves a big disservice.

I hope that when you finish reading this book, you will have had any number of "Ah Ha!" moments. I hope you will have a better understanding of the settlement process and the intricacies involved in it. You will know what you should do *before* you go in, eyes wide open. You will understand the role and responsibility each party plays, and what the process looks like from my side of the desk, and you may get an inkling of some of the strange things that can happen when all hell breaks loose. Sometimes we must look at it as a war that has to be fought on all sides. Yes, you have to fight to achieve your American dream. As in any war, knowledge is power and control. Understanding means less stress, whether it is for a buyer, a seller, a real estate agent, or even an attorney who may be involved in some form or fashion. Understanding the why means the settlement agent/escrow officer will have fewer problems getting the information she needs from the parties involved, and getting it in a timely fashion. Understanding will make the transaction go smoothly. Wouldn't it be nice to win this war with the least amount of casualties to the nerves and the pocketbook?

NO ONE LIKES TO BE MISUNDERSTOOD

There isn't another process that grabs our emotions and gets us as firmly involved as a purchase or sale of a property. Yes, it can be a very emotional process!

On the seller's side, this may be a home that has been lived in for thirty, forty or even fifty years, a home where babies were born and brought up through their school years and into adulthood. There are memories attached to this property. Letting go of it is a difficult thing.

On the buyer's side you are looking for that perfect place where you can build the memories, and of course there is the drama of putting a large chunk of money down. Once the money is put on the table, this is it!

Because there is no firm understanding of the process, customers may find that events happen totally out of their control. It can be a very frustrating exercise. You may have a real estate agent guiding you through, but does the agent really know the process? No matter how closely we work with real estate agents, I am afraid that just as I cannot relate to all that they do, they cannot explain what happens behind the settlement desk either. How can they explain the stages and steps to their clients if they themselves don't know? The whole process involves different professionals from different industries handling different parts of the process.

It is time to understand the different parts of the process and how the settlement agent ties it all together. It is time to clarify and demystify the process and, along the way, give certain tips on how to navigate the whole procedure without undue gnashing of teeth, tearing of hair or development of an ulcer. When the understanding and the knowledge is there, the stress is lessened, and that goes not only for the Mr. Wyznovskis of the world, but especially for their hardworking and long suffering escrow officers.

At this juncture I want to emphasize that as the purchase of our home can be one of the single most important events in our lives, this book is focused on the buying and selling of a single family home in California, particularly in southern California. As you will see in the next chapters, we handle different types of transactions differently. Transactions are also handled differently not only between the northern and southern part of California but also in the rest of the country. The same basic principles might apply, but the preparation, work, and timeline are different. In the end it is the purchase of our home that is the achievement of the American dream and an emotional highlight of our lives.

2

First, It's Back
to the Basics

CHAPTER TWO

First, It's Back to the Basics

ABIDING BY A CERTAIN CODE

Settlement services all have the same goal: to get a real estate transaction "closed" (completed) and finalized. But the route to that final goal is not always the same. There are different types of real estate transactions that I will touch upon in later chapters, as everything is handled just a little bit differently, depending on the transaction. The basics are the same, but the fine points differ. I will also delve into the differences between California and the rest of the country, as well as the differences between northern and southern California.

I am also going to talk about timelines a bit later. I am going to make sure that everyone has the information they need to feel confident about the process and achieve the American dream by purchasing the property they want. We want people to understand the process not only so they will feel more in control but also so they can help us do our jobs more efficiently.

Our jobs come with a special code of conduct that we must follow. We also talk a certain language, as you can see in Appendix E in the back of the book. Some of the terms I will be using are interchangeable. For instance, "escrow," as we call it in California, could be called "settlement services" elsewhere.

The escrow holder is the person or the company prepared to conduct the transaction. The escrow holder can be known as the "closing agent" or "stakeholder." The person who handles the escrow is an "escrow officer," or a "settlement agent," or a "closing agent." Different names, same function.

What is it that we actually do? The escrow process calls for the deposit of certain funds, documents, real or personal property by one party to an "impartial, neutral third party agent" for delivery to the other party once the agreement or contract between the two parties is completed. It is not solely limited to the transfer of real estate. Escrows can be used for the transfer of anything, immovable or movable.

What, then, is the code of conduct for this all-important escrow holder?

Certain aspects of the transaction itself should not be divulged to anybody but those involved in the transaction. I'm not going to let the information about the transaction go to the nosy next-door neighbor who wants to know how much the property sold for. I'm not going to indulge the curious brother-in-law who calls to ask how the transaction is going. We don't even give the IRS or the state government agencies specific information. They have to go through the proper channels and have a court order or a subpoena issued if they want to obtain information from us.

Our files are sacred and secure unless a court of law orders us to provide them. In any transaction, we ask the parties for private information: Social Security number, driver's license number, and addresses. We have to assure our clients that we are not going to allow this information to fall into other people's hands. So, first and foremost in the escrow holder's code of conduct is *confidentiality.* That is our number-one priority, and we are not going to let anything in a transaction be made public, especially personal information, even between the parties themselves.

If my seller gives me his Social Security number, I am usually the only one who sees it. Only in very special circumstances would the buyer be required to see it. If a buyer wants to see my seller's closing statement, do I show it to him? No. Just because the buyer is a party to the same transaction does not mean he is privy to all of the documents, and all of the other party's information. Only if the seller had agreed to the release of such information, would I do so. That is our code of confidentiality.

The second important code regards *impartiality.* In most transactions there are at least two parties with conflicting views. The parties' actions are based on an agreement that they hammered out at the beginning when everything was so exciting and full of hope. But things happen, and the contract drawn up in the beginning may be subject to events outside a person's control. Let's take the case of my sellers the Kessingers and my buyers the Cheungs.

During an inspection conducted at the beginning of the transaction, it was found that extensive repair work was required, and the Kessingers agreed to do it. But the day before the closing, the Cheungs conducted their final walk-through inspection and found that the repair work had been done in a poor and shoddy manner. All of the funds were in, and all of the documents were signed, but the Cheungs refused to allow the transaction to close, and they submitted a written notification to escrow to stop the closing. The Kessingers, however, demanded that the closing continue. What does the escrow holder do?

Because we are a neutral third party, we are impartial to either side, and this impartiality calls for us to put everything on hold until the issues between the two parties are resolved. We are not allowed to take sides, as losing our impartiality would mean the loss of our fiduciary responsibilities to both sides.

If the impasse continues, the Kessingers and the Cheungs may call the escrow holder for advice: What should they do? What is their legal recourse? The third code of conduct is that there shall be *no legal advice given.* Legal advice, as we all know, should be given only by those who have passed their bar exam and are allowed to practice law. Anyone else giving such advice or practicing law (especially those who are put in a "trust" capacity like escrow holders) will subject themselves to serious legal consequences if the advice they give is detrimental, or contrary to law.

The Kessingers and the Cheungs were able to work out their differences, and the agreement on how to continue was recorded in instructions. So the fourth code of conduct for the escrow holder is to act only upon receipt of *mutually agreed-upon written instructions.* This is very important. You will see in later chapters that our governing agency looks at our files and makes sure everything we have done is transacted according to mutually agreed instructions.

One more thing that applies to our code of conduct is that we have a *limited agency relationship* with both of the parties. This relationship means that the escrow holder has a fiduciary responsibility to the parties and is bound to act as their agent within the context of, and for the purposes of, fulfilling the parties' instructions. This relationship ends when the transaction is closed. However, should any issues discovered in the future point directly back to the time the transaction was handled, the agency relationship would still bind the escrow holder to her actions in the transaction.

IT'S ALL ABOUT TRUST

Elias and Anna Martinez found the perfect home, one that would be their springboard to their new family. A standard three-bedroom, two-bath house. It was in a quiet neighborhood within a good school district. They had one three-year-old daughter and another baby on the way.

John and Joanna Stewart were in their early seventies. They had their eye on a property in Palm Springs, where they could retire and be close to their youngest son. They had raised this son and two other children in this house and they had very fond memories. More importantly, this house would be their springboard to their new home because all of the equity they had accumulated in it would more than pay for their new home. Plus it would provide a nice little nest egg for them to live on.

Real estate agents handled the transaction for the parties, who never actually met each other. The Martinezes wanted to be sure that when they handed over their chunk of money, they would have ownership of the home but not be stuck with the Stewarts' debts and loans. The Stewarts, on the other hand, did not want to sign over ownership until they had the Martinezes' money in hand. There was, in fact, *a lack of trust*. And it was because of this lack of trust that a whole new industry was formed.

According to *Merriam Webster's New Collegiate Dictionary*, ninth edition, "escrow" is "a deed, a bond, money, or a piece of property held in trust by a third party to be turned over to the grantee only upon the fulfillment of a condition." What the Martinezes and Stewarts needed was a third party. This third party would hold on to the money and the deed to the property. This third party would make sure the loans belonging to the Stewarts were paid off. This third party would make sure the Martinezes' new loan was secured on the property. This third party would make sure that all of the other pre-agreed conditions were fulfilled. Then, and only then would the money and title exchange take place: the Martinezes would get the ownership deed and the Stewarts would get their money. To get to that end result they would enter into an escrow with this third party.

But that is not all.

AND TO PROVIDE AN ACCOUNTING

Remember, what we term "escrow" in California is also called "settlement services" here and in other parts of the nation. The important word is "settlement"—as in "settling the account." We settle the account for the parties.

Let's go back to the Kessingers and the Cheungs. The Kessingers had used their property to secure two loans on it: the first, a standard thirty-year loan, and the second, an equity line of credit. All of this came out when a search of records of the title was conducted, and further corroborated by the Kessingers.

What also came out of the search, which these sellers were not aware of at the time, was that there were two other liens attached to the property. One was a judgment that had been filed against Mr. Kessinger by a partner in a partnership gone sour. The other was a personal property tax lien that had been filed by the county tax collector's office on unpaid taxes at a location separate from our property but listing Mr. Kessinger's name.

Both the judgment and the tax lien were personal debts, and in California, certain debts of this nature have a life span of ten years. Once filed against a person's name, a lien automatically attaches to everything that person owns at the time or could possibly own in the future. As I tell my clients, it's like a particularly virulent computer virus that infects all of the programs it comes in contact with. You have to get rid of it, or you can't move forward in life.

A standard contract for the purchase of a home normally calls for the buyer to receive ownership of the property clear of all of the seller's liens. Because I am the third-party settlement agent holding all of the money and documents, it becomes my responsibility to find out just how much is owed on the liens. In addition, I have to pay bills and invoices from outside vendors contracted to do work in relation to the sale. Was there structural pest control (termite) repair work? Were there contractor or handyman bills for other repairs? Is the property part of a condominium or townhome complex with a homeowners association? All of these bills, debts, and liens have to be paid, and most of them are paid by me, the escrow holder.

On the other hand, Mr. and Mrs. Cheung also had their own bills that had to be paid by the escrow holder. The biggest was the cost for the new loan they were obtaining. Loan origination, document fees, and other lender charges have to be paid as well as a full year's home insurance premium.

The second reason to have an escrow, then, is to make sure the third party will "settle the accounts" at the end and provide a copy of the settlement. For the buyers, the Cheungs, the settlement statement would show the purchase price, what they paid to get their loan, the other costs such as insurance, association dues, and government recording fees, and, of course, the costs for handling the escrow. To balance the cost side, the settlement statement also shows the down-payment funds brought in by the Cheungs as well as the amount of the new loan that the lender gave for the purchase.

For the sellers, the Kessingers, the settlement statement would show that from the sales price the following deductions were made: the two loans secured on the property, the final amount on the judgment, and the personal property taxes, which, it turned out, were unpaid taxes belonging to that business partnership that fell through. Because the agreement between the Kessingers and the Cheungs was that the Kessingers would pay for termite and repair work, the bills for those were also deducted from the Kessingers' account, as was their share of the escrow costs. Once the deductions were made, what was left of the sales price became the final proceeds they received from the sale of their home.

The term "settlement services" comes from the escrow officer's role as a third-party clearinghouse for the payment of liens, debts,  and bills related to the transaction, and as a provider of a statement outlining in exact detail those costs paid on the customer's behalf—*to the penny.* This settlement statement is used for income tax purposes and is given to the buyer's new lender to prove that everything that was contracted for was carried out and paid for.

But that is still not all.

AND THEN THERE ARE THOSE OTHER IMPORTANT REASONS . . .

In the old days two parties would get together, talk, shake hands, and that was it. But today, when litigation is resorted to at any sign of the slightest conflict, things do not happen simply on a handshake. So, if no real estate agents are involved and a standard real estate contract is not drawn up, what happens?

As we tell our for-sale-by-owner clients, the instructions they give us on everything they have agreed to become their binding contract and recognized under contract law. So the escrow instructions I prepare become not only your instructions to me on what needs to happen but also the agreement between yourselves as to what you must follow. It is the "map" of the transaction, from the starting point to the end point. Like a game of Monopoly, you pass "Go," you collect $200, and you get to buy the property. I actually have a large poster of Park Place and Boardwalk hanging in the office as a reminder of the name of our game.

One of the important guarantees that a seller can give a buyer in a purchase of real property is the guarantee of *clear title*, just the way the buyer wants it. The guarantee comes in the form of *title insurance*. The topic of title insurance could be a whole book by itself, written by a title officer with his own thirty-five years or more in the industry. For this book, suffice it to say that we handle the purchase of a title insurance policy, a policy that you can depend on if certain issues concerning your ownership come into doubt after the transaction is completed. In order to issue title insurance, the escrow holder has to contract out to a title company and give that company express instructions as to the exact type of policy required for the particular transaction.

The lender, who puts down a huge chunk of money, also has demands for its own policy of title insurance. It is up to the escrow officer to make sure that the demands of both the buyer and the lender are met and the right type of title insurance is purchased.

In California there are certain licenses, in particular, liquor licenses, that require an escrow holder to process the transfer according to government code . Normally, the transfer of the license is attached to the sale of the restaurant where the license is parked. So this is another answer to "why escrow?"—the *transfer of a particular type of license* according to government regulations so that the new owner does not inherit the debts or taxes of the old owner.

One final reason a person might need an escrow holder is for the *satisfactory sale* and delivery of certain personal property—goods, documents, or personal items. If you are selling a nice piece of art for a large amount of money, would you deliver the artwork if the

purchase funds were not in your account? Vice versa, would you fork out thousands of dollars if you did not have the artwork in hand?

So, we come back to that one word: *trust.*

WE ARE NOT ALL ALIKE

In California there are various types of settlement agents, and we are all governed differently by different government agencies.

The concept of settlement services is the same throughout the United States, and the code that settlement agents are guided by should also be the same. But the types of companies that can offer settlement services are different, and in California they are governed by different government jurisdictions. Here's how it works.

Independent escrow companies—"Independents" as we call ourselves—are corporations established for the sole purpose of handling settlement services. Independents are governed by the State of California's Department of Corporations (DOC). My company is one of those "Independents."

Independents are subject to full background checks, licensing, bonding, and asset liquidity requirements. Every single individual we hire must submit fingerprints for intensive background checks with the State of California Department of Justice. Any hint of state or federal criminal records may make a person non-hireable. Because we handle huge amounts of funds for the general public, the DOC imposes strict rules and guidelines about conduct, the escrow process, and the handling of these funds. After all, millions of dollars could be passing through our accounts on any given day.

Besides yearly audits by certified public accountants, Independents are also subject to a DOC audit at least every four years. After all, this is your money; we have a duty to protect it and handle it with care.

The auditors check everything, including every penny we have disbursed, the documentation for the disbursement of that penny, and the accounting not only of our customer's trust account but also our own corporate account. The auditors want to be sure that we are not receiving kickbacks, paying referral fees, or doing something that is fraudulent or illegal. If anything untoward is found, they immediately shut the company down with a cease and desist order, and appoint a conservator to handle all of the trust funds. Boom. They close our doors, no ifs, ands, or buts. This is the protection given to consumers dealing with Independents. We are monitored by a very strict regulatory agency.

Title company escrow departments—"Title Escrow" is our short name for those escrow departments that work under a title insurance company's umbrella. California's title insurance companies are governed under California's Department of Insurance (DOI) and so their escrow departments would fall under the DOI's jurisdiction also.

The main focus of title insurance companies and the DOI is on the title insurance side of the business, not the settlement services, even though they are intimately tied together. Unlike other areas of the country where settlement services can be handled solely by title insurance companies, in California it is a side-line, a by-product of the main business. Title Escrows are not stand-alone as the Independents are. Some of the large title insurance companies have a business relationship with certain financial institutions to handle their foreclosure work so the settlement-services part of said transactions are automatically handled by that title company's escrow department as an extension of its existing title business. Interestingly you might have a transaction in which the settlement services are handled by ABC title company and the title insurance is handled by XYZ title company. One transaction with two title companies involved, one handling the escrow, one handling the title insurance. That is how it can work in California sometimes.

Real estate Broker Owned escrow departments—"Broker Owned" is the short name for those escrow departments that work under a real estate broker's license and are governed under California's Department of Real Estate (DRE). As with the title insurance companies, the escrow business is not its main focus, just a side-line that brings in additional income. Broker Owned are limited in that they can only take a transaction in which at least one of the sides of the transaction is represented by a licensed real estate broker from that same office.

The concern in a transaction handled by a Broker Owned escrow is that the neutrality of the settlement agent can be compromised. If you are handling a transaction with a real estate broker from your own company on one end and another real estate broker from another company on the other end, who do you listen to when there is a conflict? Are you going to listen to your broker, your colleague, your office mate, or are you going to listen to the other broker? Where is the neutrality?

The Broker Owned escrow departments are easy to set up and close down, requiring no special licensing, bonding, or even office space separate from the real estate business. These concerns have led to a lack of accountability.

Other entities—I first started in this industry thirty-some years ago, when I worked at a bank. At that time settlement services were handled mostly by escrow departments within banks. Today the banking industry has given up this type of service as it concentrates on other financial products that make much more money.

Many old-time escrow officers will tell you that they came from a banking background, such as Bank of America, Security Pacific National Bank, and so on. These banks were the training ground for escrow officers way back when, and you could rely on those people to be strict professionals trained in the traditional way. No short cuts! We (and yes, I am one of those, so I am just slightly prejudiced) started by typing everything on typewriters, balancing the file, and doing all of the calculations by hand. Of course, a purchase contract in those days was just one page, whereas today it is a minimum of eight pages! Today everything is done on a computer and as long as you have the right software and you hit the right button, the computer will figure it all out for you.

Besides banks, attorneys in California are also allowed to handle settlement services, but that is very rare. It is a matter of fact that some attorneys rely on good escrow officers to handle their transactions and provide answers to some of the questions they have with respect to the settlement process. Things are different on the East Coast, where many states have attorneys in control of the settlement process.

So, although there are a number of different types of entities that handle settlement services, the commonality lies in the following functions:

Confidentiality of the transaction

Neutrality of the third-party stakeholder

No imparting of *legal advice*

Precise and correct *accounting* of all funds held in trust

Performance through *mutual instructions* given by only the parties involved

What is important to note is that we are not alike. Depending on what settlement service entity you have chosen, the governing guidelines may go from very strict to almost nonexistent.

It is imperative for the clients to understand that this could be an important factor in the handling and sanctity of the transaction as a whole.

IT'S NOT JUST HOMES

Nope, it's not just single family homes (SFR), although that is what comes to most people's minds when I talk about a sale escrow transaction. That's because, if my business is any indication, as of 2012 a good 70 percent of sales business comes from owner-occupied homes (whether as a standard purchase, an REO, or a short sale). The rest is a combination of income property, commercial, vacant land, or business. And I am not even counting our refinance business.

There is a specific breakdown of the term "property":

1. **Real property.** The bulk of our work comes from the purchase/sale of real property, which is defined as immovable land and the improvements that are attached to it.

   Residential:

   A *single family residence* that sits on its own piece of land; ownership of both the structure and the land is tied together. This is a property which you can build or tear down to your heart's content, as long as it is done with the approval of the planning and building department of the particular city where the property is located. You can paint the house any color you want or let it deteriorate or fall apart if you want, and unless it becomes an eye sore or a nuisance, no one can do anything about it. You enjoy *absolute ownership without limitation.*

A *condominium unit* is a home that is part of a condominium project, normally attached to other units, sharing a wall and a continuous roofline. A condominium project can be one story or a high rise. Ownership of a condominium unit is known for what it *does not* include, and that is the land on which the building stands, the actual structure itself, and the common area of the project. Ownership consists of only the living space within the walls of the unit.

Restrictions are placed on what the individual homeowners can or cannot do to the outside of the unit. The common area, land, and buildings are all set up to be owned by an association for the benefit of all of the owners of the complex. The association maintains and governs the whole complex. You can paint the inside of your unit whatever bright purple color you want, but any painting, addition, or repair of the outside of the unit has to follow guidelines established by the homeowner association.

It is important that the restrictions, conditions, rules, regulations, and financial statements of the association be provided to the buyer for review early in the transaction in case the buyer finds issue with anything. Ownership of a condominium unit is the *individual ownership of air space within the unit and collective ownership of the rest.*

A *townhouse* unit is also part of a large complex but detached and standing alone. The owner owns the structure and the land it sits on, but there are common areas that exist for the benefit of all of the owners. They each own a share of the common area. Like a condominium, a townhouse is part of a larger project that has restrictions as to what an owner can or cannot do to the outside the structure. Again, association documents must be given to the buyer early in the process for his approval. This type of property entails *individual ownership of the structure and the land it stands on and collective ownership of the common area.*

Apartment units are simply one structure separated into distinct living quarters that are then rented out by the owner/landlord. The owner has absolute ownership without limitation. The individual units cannot be sold or transferred individually. When handling apartment buildings, we need to disclose tenant rental information at the opening of the transaction, and rents are prorated (each party gets their share) at the closing.

There are some apartment units that can be converted to condominium units and reclassified as a *condo conversion.* The now-converted individual units can be sold off individually. The conversion is a long-drawn-out process that includes going through the subdivision of the original land, approved by the city and the California Department of Real Estate.

One type of development that is very popular nowadays is a *mixed-use complex,* which combines residential condominiums on the upper levels and commercial stores on the bottom.

Mobile homes or "manufactured homes" are homes that may or may not be fixed to the land. When they are not fixed to the land, they are handled as "personal property" and the transfers go through the California Department of Housing and Community Development (HCD). Once a mobile home is fixed to a foundation that is attached to the land, it becomes a standard single family residence and is handled the same way.

One distinct difference between a structure that stands alone and one that is part of a project or complex with common areas and an owner association is the requirement of extra fees or dues, to be paid on a monthly or quarterly basis. The dues are for the maintenance and upkeep of the property, including the common areas (swimming pools, tennis courts, recreation centers, walkways, driveways, landscaping, etc.)

As a side note, with the crash of the market and the steady rise of foreclosures over the past five years, homeowners who have been "underwater" and unable to pay their mortgages normally do not pay their monthly association dues either. The bank may foreclose on the property and take it back to resell, but the homeowner association is rarely able to do that. Many, many associations have fallen on very hard times as their owners have been unable to keep up with the payment of dues, and, as a result, the associations' coffers have run dry. Loss of dues and monthly income means that maintenance and upkeep by the association falls by the wayside and only the bare minimum is done. As the project becomes dilapidated, the value of the units plummets. As the value plummets, the owners find it more difficult to sell or even refinance. It is a vicious cycle.

Commercial:

This classification includes anything that is not used for residential purposes. This could include office buildings, high rises, shopping malls, and so forth. Ownership is absolute without limitation as long as the property is not part of a commercial condominium project. Again, there may be leases to review and approve, and amounts to prorate at closing. Commercial transactions normally have a long inspection and review period, as there are many aspects of the building and its ownership that the buyer reviews: leases, income and expense, loss, and rent history. Although the providing and review of this information (called "due diligence") takes place outside the purview of the settlement agent, it is still an important step in the whole process. *Commercial condominiums* are like their residential condominium counterparts, but they must be used for commercial purposes only.

Vacant land:

This is land with nothing on it but dirt. You would think this would be the easiest to handle, and it is, except that there is also a longer-than-normal due diligence period (sometimes over a year!) during which the buyer makes all of his inspections with all of the government agencies to ascertain if his intended use will be approved. Sometimes the sale of the vacant land may come with plans and drawings that the seller

THE ART OF ESCROW

had already drawn up, and although that is "personal property," it is not normally handled separately.

I have listed the various types of real property that may be purchased/sold. Whether the property is a $10,000 piece of vacant land in the desert, a small $100,000 home in the Lancaster/Palmdale area of Los Angeles County, or a $10,000,000 home in Beverly Hills, the process of transfer is the same. The addition of a couple of zeros to the left of the decimal point does not change the process.

2. **Business Property**. Settlement services are also needed when the item being sold is an ongoing business. This is called a "bulk sale" or a "business opportunity" sale. When you are selling a business, you are selling certain tangible and intangible items. The furniture, fixtures, and equipment used in the operation of the business are part of the tangible items, which also include pots, pans, dishes, flatware, ovens, refrigerators, office furniture, computers, telephone systems, and so forth. Inventory can also be included.

The intangible items are the "goodwill," including customer lists, phone numbers, or anything that makes the business what it is but is not quantifiable. Do you have a donut shop you want to get rid of? How about an optometry business? Or a restaurant? How about an after-school tutoring business? Under California's Bulk Sale law, anything worth more than $10,000 and less than $2 million requires certain processes to be followed, and they are normally done through an escrow transaction.

Or course, we can handle anything that falls outside these parameters too.

The processing of a bulk sale is completely different from that of a real property sale. Instead of a title insurance company issuing a search and a title policy, we conduct the search directly with the California Secretary of State's office. We also publish the sale in newspapers for the benefit of vendors who might be owed money. There is no issuance of a policy of title insurance, and there are always the matters of a landlord and the premises lease to be resolved. Instead of using a deed to transfer ownership, we use a bill of sale.

If the business is being sold together with the real property on which it is situated, it has to be handled in two different processes so that it meets the guidelines and conditions of both real and business transactions.

3. **Personal Property.** As mentioned in a previous chapter, settlement services can also be called for when other personal property items are being sold. This can include anything that is moveable: cars, boats, art pieces, livestock and inventory, or the satisfactory delivery of goods, documents, and so forth. The way to handle these transactions really depends on the property being sold. A car or boat may need to incorporate the transfer of the license through the California Department of Motor Vehicles. The delivery of goods may require a bill of lading. When you have livestock, you may even need health department certifications and a manual head count or "countdown" on the day of the closing.

4. **Holding escrows:** Do you need a neutral third party to hold funds pending the satisfactory completion of certain conditions? This type of a transaction is usually called a "holding escrow." An example of this is a "funds control" escrow in which construction funds are set aside for disbursement, pending the work being done, and submission of ticketed invoices from the contractor.

5. **License transfers.** There is one type of license transfer that requires the involvement of a settlement agent. The California Department of Alcoholic Beverage Control (ABC) requires that an escrow be opened for the transfer of a liquor license. The reason for that is simple: the ABC has very strict guidelines on who can sell liquor. An application for a liquor license takes time, as a full background check with the Department of Justice is required. No money can go from buyer to seller until the ABC says "Go." So they "trust" (here is that word again!) that the escrow holder is in control of the funds, and the transaction will not proceed until the Department of Alcoholic Beverage Control gives the final word.

6. **Refinances.** We all remember the refinance craze from 2004 to 2007 that brought about the worldwide economic crash. In California, if you are planning to refinance your home or real property, chances are you will be required to open an escrow for the transaction. The lender will (1) require title insurance to be issued—and to get this insurance an escrow has to be opened, (2) ask the escrow holder to review the ownership of the property to make

sure that the borrower is the owner, (3) require that all liens and debts that need to be paid are paid, and (4) require a settlement statement.

You might ask why a refinance requires a neutral third party. Well, a refinance also involves two parties, a borrower and a lender who don't trust each other. So yes, where there is no trust, there is no way.

RELATIONSHIPS MATTER

There are usually four industry players (outside our actual buyer and seller) in a given transaction and it is an intimate relationship that we all share:

- The real estate industry
- The title insurance industry
- The mortgage and lending industry
- The settlement services (escrow) industry

Do we need each other? Sure we do, but in varying degrees. Let me explain the process first.

In order to sell a property, do the seller and buyer need these four industries to get involved with the sale? Actually, no.

John Doe sells to Richard Smith a property on 123 Main Street for $50,000. These are men of the Old West tradition, in which a man's word and handshake are as binding as any modern legal agreement. John picks up a grant deed form from the local stationary store, fills it out to the best of his ability, and has it

notarized. When Richard gives him a check for the $50,000, John hands over the deed.

Did the property ownership transfer? Yes, it did. The fact that John signed the deed and handed it to Richard in exchange for money completed the transaction.

Of course, if it were this simple, those aforementioned four industries could not have become such huge businesses. And have I seen this scenario happen? Yes, I have, but let me tell you, it was not pretty for Richard.

Let's see how the process evolves when these four industries are included. The function of the real estate broker is to help John market his property, to sell it for the highest price he can, and to find the best property for Richard to buy at the lowest price available. If all of the stars align and it's fated to be, the finalized contract between John and Richard is given to the settlement agent to process.

The settlement agent will then contract with the title insurance provider to obtain title insurance on 123 Main Street. They first issue a report on the property and check to see if John Doe has any other outstanding liens against him personally. The report needs to show what is present and accounted for on the ownership of the property—restrictions and rights to the building, ownership, and liens against the property and against John himself. This report gives us a general idea of what we are dealing with. If it is clean, wonderful. If not, the settlement agent rolls up her shirt sleeves and gets to work. At the end of the transaction the title insurance company issues a clean policy of title insurance for Richard's benefit to confirm his ownership just the way he wanted it.

If Richard needed a loan to meet the purchase price, he would have contacted his loan officer who would have worked with the settlement agent. The loan officer would have provided the loan documents for Richard to sign, and once signed, the loan officer would have sent the loan funds to the settlement agent to complete the transaction.

Every step of the way the four parties are in close contact with each other. "Teamwork" is the one word we use, and "communication" is the other.

In the original scenario, none of the four parties were needed, but is that such a good idea? In a for-sale-by-owner (FSBO) transaction, the real estate broker doesn't come into the equation. In a cash transaction for which no loan is needed, the loan officer's services are not required.

If you are willing to forego title insurance, which protects and defends you from any ghosts that may arise due to John's past ownership, you won't need a title company.

And if the buyer and seller have ultimate trust in each other, they probably won't care if there is no settlement agent involved.

And here is the crux of the matter: the importance of what I, the settlement agent, do for you. If I am not handling your transaction, where is the professional who will make sure that all the t's are crossed and i's dotted? Who will make sure that all the federal, state, and local laws or ordinances regarding the sale are followed? Who will make sure that John Doe really owns the property and all of his loans are paid? If you are willing to take the risk and just do a handshake and hand over the money, I guess you won't need the settlement agent either.

Like everything else in life and business, it's all about relationships. Real estate, mortgage, and title, and escrow have a symbiotic relationship, but they each have their own function to perform in the whole. If everyone performs well, we will have a happy buyer and seller. If there is a clog anywhere, the domino effect could make it a disaster and bring a tremendous amount of stress to the buyer and seller.

I am a settlement agent so it's natural that I should elevate my importance, but still, Appendix A in the back of this book, titled "Escrow, in the Center of Things," shows that we are indeed in the center, juggling all of the balls and pulling it all together.

One more thing: As a buyer or seller, you are the consumer and you have rights that you can exercise. The most important right is the one of *choice*. Exercise your right of choice when choosing the real estate broker, title insurance company, mortgage/lender, and settlement agent.

Tip: Some real estate companies own their own mortgage, settlement and even title insurance companies. By law they must disclose if they have interests in these other companies. Allowing all the services to be handled in-house may interfere with the code of neutrality. Be sure you know if your providers have affiliated interests that might conflict with yours.

LOCATION, LOCATION, LOCATION

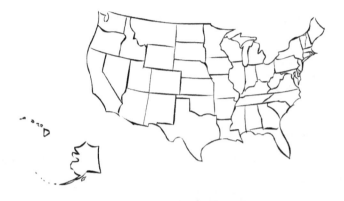

We know that the basics of handling settlement services are pretty much the same everywhere. But the type of entity that handles the services varies from state to state, and from region to region. The breakdown and payment of costs can be different too. The types of documents that are used to transfer ownership—grant deed, warranty deed, bargain and sale deed—or to secure loans may also be different. We will just touch on a few states here in different regions. This information is taken from "Real Estate Practices—State by State," issued by First American Title Insurance Company.

1. Western states
   - California—there are slight differences between the practices handled in the north and the south of California. In the north, transactions are handled mostly through Title Escrows, and in the south they are handled through Independents, Title Escrows, or Broker Owned.
   - Oregon—escrow companies are used as well as attorneys.
   - Washington—there are differences between east and west. In eastern Washington, attorneys handle settlement services,

and in western Washington it can be title companies, independents, escrow agents, lenders, or attorneys.

- Arizona—title companies and title agents.
- Nevada—their practices are similar to California, and escrow companies are used.

2. Eastern states

- Florida—attorneys and title companies if title insurance is required.
- Louisiana—it's a little different here. Attorneys and corporate title agents are used, and the process requires a notary public who must authenticate the documents.
- Maine—attorneys.
- New Jersey—attorneys.
- New York—attorneys. New York is known for its "round table closing" in which all parties and their attorneys meet on the day of closing at a designated closing attorney's office and sit around the table signing paperwork and passing funds, all at the same time.
- North Carolina—attorneys.
- Pennsylvania—title companies, title agents, or approved attorneys.
- Virginia—attorneys and sometimes title companies.

3. Central states

- Arkansas—attorneys and title agents.
- Colorado—title companies.
- Idaho—escrow agents.
- Illinois—title companies, lenders and attorneys, with attorneys preparing the real estate documents.

- Minnesota—title companies, lenders, real estate agents and attorneys, with the parties represented at the table by their own legal counsel.
- Texas—title companies.

4. Other areas:
   - Alaska—title companies, escrow companies, and lenders. Alaska is very different, and the handling of the sale of land has to go through the federal government to conform to the federal government's Native Allotment Act and because much of the land was originally purchased from Russia.
   - Hawaii—title companies and escrow companies, but attorneys handle the preparation of real estate documents. Hawaii is also very different because most of the land is held in lease form.

Can we handle transactions across California state lines? Yes we can, as long as the particular state allows it and documents that are necessary for mortgage or ownership transfer are drawn correctly on the form that is used in that state.

In refinance transactions in which the lender is drawing the mortgage documents and following Fannie Mae or Freddie Mac document standards, Independents and Title Escrows, can also handle transactions in other states. This is of particular convenience to our clients who reside in California but own other income property or second homes in other states.

3

Before We Get to the Table

CHAPTER THREE

Before We Get to the Table

YOUR GREATEST STRENGTH: PREPARATION

Let's say you are baking a cake. First you decide what kind of a cake you are going to make. You look up the recipe and review it, step by step. You look over the ingredients, check out your pantry for what you need, and go to the market if you find that there is something you don't have. You put it all on the counter, and then you start. You turn on the oven to the correct temperature. Once everything is in the pan, you put it in oven where it cooks for a certain predetermined period of time. The oven bell dings, you pull the final product out, and you serve your masterpiece to an appreciative family. *Voila!*

It's almost the same for every real estate purchase transaction. You start with the decision to sell/buy. You look at what you need to get started. You put it all on the countertop in the form of an agreement. The settlement agent is your oven in which you deposit the agreement and you let it cook. When the predetermined time is reached, the transaction is finalized and the final product is rolled out. I want to buy; you want to sell, or simply said: end result (price) = ingredients (conditions) + time. Most important is to make sure the ingredients that are thrown into the mix are correct. This means that both buyers and sellers have to look at the ingredients and do their homework *before* they get to that point.

THE SELLER: "I AM GOING TO ASK FOR THE WORLD"

As a seller, I will inevitably ask for the world, or the world according to my definition. If the property is my primary asset, I will definitely squeeze every last drop from it.

John and Joanna Stewart, whom we met in Chapter Two, lived in their property for more than forty years. Although they had fond memories of the place, it needed a lot of maintenance and repairs.

They had an idea of how much a new home in the Palm Springs area was going to cost. They knew that they didn't owe any money on their present house, and they knew they would have to get a great

offer on it. Putting all of their emotions aside (and yes, there were a lot of emotions when they were looking at their home and thinking of all of the wonderful memories associated with it), they realized that the maintenance issues they had put off through the years had to be taken care of so that the house would attract a good buyer. So Mr. and Mrs. Stewart took a step back and looked, really looked, at the house from a third-party perspective. They realized that they needed to consider the "curb appeal" of their home, to plant flowers, fix the fence, and give the inside and outside a brand-new coat of paint.

Here are the ingredients that the seller needs to put on the counter:

1. What am I using the sale proceeds for? Do I need it to buy another place? Do I know how much money I will need to complete the other transaction?

2. If I don't own my home free and clear, what are the loans and debts I need to pay off?

Tip: Pull out your monthly mortgage statements and jot down the unpaid balances.

---

3. What are my transaction costs? Call your escrow officer for a quote. Ask her for a detail of all costs, not just her escrow charges. An estimation is better than nothing.

4. Contact third-party vendors for repair quotes. Termite repair work is a big issue in California where structures are almost all made of wood, and termite infestation can happen even in a new construction.

5. Once you have a handle on the debit side of the column, you will need to fill in the credit side, and you must ask yourself what you think the value of your home is.

6. Not everyone has a real estate agent to help with ascertaining a good market value, but a seller (and a buyer) can come up with a figure by checking online tools at sites such as www.Zillow.com, or http://realestate.yahoo.com/home-worth, or Google "market value."

The Stewarts did their mental homework and their physical homework by repairing, repainting, and replanting *before* they put up the for-sale sign. Sure, they were going to ask the world for their house, but they also had a *realistic* view of what their net result was going to be. They did not want any surprises, which would definitely affect their ability to buy that Palm Springs home.

Tip: When you are set on selling your property ask a settlement agent to start the process and order a preliminary search report on your property, and run all the owners' names through the general index.

Just as they did with the personal credit report, all sellers should check to see if there are any unknown issues affecting the ownership of their property. I urge everyone to obtain a "property profile" or "chain of title" report from a title company, and incorporate in the report any findings on the general index against the owners. This will prevent any surprises coming up during the transaction, which might entail receiving a frantic phone call from your escrow officer.

There are too many cases of white-collar crime these days. Crooks steal your name and identity and use your property to obtain hundreds and thousands of dollars from unsuspecting lenders, leaving you and your property on the brink of foreclosure when payments on the fraudulent loan are not made. Check your property ownership every so many years to make sure you are not a victim of identity theft.

WHEREAS, FOR THE BUYER: "HOW LOW CAN I GO?"

In my more than thirty years in the business I have seen many, many types of buyers. There is the logical buyer, the emotional buyer, the organized buyer, the disorganized buyer, the very much distracted buyer, and every type in between. Every one of them has the same thought, "how low can I go and still have the seller accept my offer?"

Before we even go there, let's take a look at which ingredients the buyer needs to lay on the counter:

1. First and foremost, is this an *impulse buy?* If so, you are probably going to experience buyer's remorse when you open the transaction, start to feel doubts and back out. All of that work for nothing!

2. Do you know where you would like to purchase? What are your needs? Close to public transportation? Close to markets? Walking distance to schools? Do you need to look into the school district? All of this will narrow down your scope. If you are working with a real estate agent this is valuable information that he or she will need.

3. Do you have a clear picture of your family's finances, and will they allow you to make this purchase? You might think

this is a redundant question, but in uncertain economic times that extra credit card bill, that extra car repair bill, and less overtime, can all affect your bottom line.

4. If you are getting a loan, what does your credit report look like? Are there things on it that should be cleaned out before the loan officer gets a copy? Get an idea of what it looks like and what items can be eliminated to make your score higher. You can consciously increase or decrease your credit score. Applying for credit cards is one way of lowering it, as is applying for other types of credit, such as auto, mortgage, or personal loans. Every time an inquiry is made regarding your credit rating, your score goes down. There are also *unconscious acts that may have far-reaching consequences, such as forgetting to pay bills, and throwing mail (bills) away without looking at them. Here are three credit agencies you can use:* www.TransUnion.com, www. Equifax.com, www.Experian.com.

Tip: Take advantage of the free yearly credit report. Don't wait until someone else pulls it up when you are in the middle of loan processing.

---

5. Have you chosen a loan officer yet? This should be done even before you have settled on a property to buy so that

this person has time to clean up your application quickly and point out issues that may need to be resolved before it goes into escrow.

6. How much monthly payment can you afford? It's not just the principal and interest; you need to include taxes and insurance for a more realistic figure. All of this needs to be considered against a backdrop of your normal and regular monthly expenses.

7. How much cash do you have for your down payment?

8. What are the transaction costs you will need to add on to the down-payment amount? Call both your loan officer and your escrow officer for a quote. Ask them for details of all costs, not just their own charges.

9. Is part of your down payment coming from others? Tell your loan officer. All of the funds that you are using have to be traced and aged.

10. Is part of the funds coming from the sale of another property? If so, how is that transaction coming along? (Refer to the seller's section: "I Am Going to Ask for the World")

11. Are all the funds in the correct bank accounts, and has the information been given to the loan officer?

Tired yet? It's exhausting, isn't it?

12. Did you figure in a few months reserve funds after all is said and done? The lender will require this, but it is also for your own benefit.

13. How much will property taxes be each year? These can take a huge chunk out of your reserve funds.

14. Do not do anything that will affect your credit after you enter into this transaction. Don't buy a car; don't change a job; and of course, remain employed.

15. How do you take title? As an individual? Under a trust? As an LLC? How about a limited partnership or corporation? Decisions, decisions, decisions. If taking title as an individual, you need to think about vesting. Will ownership be a joint tenancy, or will it be community property (California community property laws)? Take a look at our Appendices D-1 and D-2, which show you ways in which you can take and vest your title.

Tip: The manner of taking title has tax consequences, especially after death. If you are obtaining a new loan, taking title other than as an individual will create more underwriting issues. Besides checking with your legal and financial counsel before you open escrow, you may want to check with your loan officer to see what additional paperwork the lender will require.

---

16. Doing a comparison study in the area where you want to purchase is an especially good idea. Use www.zillow.com or http://realestate.yahoo.com/home-worth or Google "market value."

If you are using a real estate agent, he will help you generate comparables for your analysis. This will give you an idea of how low you can go without getting kicked off the negotiating table.

Armed with the above, you can now present an offer for purchase when the right house comes up. So it won't be just "how low can I go?" but also "how high can I fly?" You will know your bottom line and upper limit and this will make for a much smoother transaction.

Once both sides have completed their check lists, they will then get down to the nitty-gritty of making and accepting an offer.

Now, you may ask why Juliana put in this whole presale chapter. What does it have to do with the actual settlement service? The answer is simple. The more you are prepared in every aspect, the less the surprises, the less the trauma. Like baking a cake, all of the ingredients have to be correct or the cake will not come out!

4

What Can I Expect in a Transaction?

CHAPTER FOUR

What Can I Expect in a Transaction?

TIME FOR THE NITTY-GRITTY!

In the excitement of finalizing the deal and being able to "open" (definition: begin, proceed with, start) the transaction, buyers, sellers, and real estate agents often forget to provide certain vital information that will allow the settlement agents to properly start the process. Sometimes the information given may prompt us to ask additional questions, which may then lead to some head scratching or scrambling for better answers, or, even worse, may become an obstacle not previously realized!

THE CONTRACT

Is there a purchase agreement or contract signed between parties? This contract does not have to be a real estate contract form as provided by the real estate industry; it can be just a hand-drawn agreement. Whatever it is, provide it to the settlement agent.

Here are the basics of what we are looking for, and if they aren't there, we will ask for them, and once we incorporate them into our escrow instructions, the contract becomes binding when it is signed:

- Purchase price
- Down-payment amount
- New loan amount
- Earnest money (initial good-faith) deposit, if any
- Duration of transaction
- What conditions are agreed upon between parties?

If the transaction is a for-sale-by-owner (FSBO) transaction, it is recommended that both buyer and seller come to the settlement agent's office to discuss what to put into the contract.

If there are real estate agents involved, the agents usually communicate with the settlement agent. No matter which scenario takes place, the requirements to open a transaction smoothly remain the same.

CORRECT PROPERTY ADDRESS

Settlement agents don't actually go to look at the property, so the confirmation of the property address is important. This is of special importance when the property sold is one unit of a new condominium/townhouse complex. Do the door numbers match the legal numbers marked on the condominium plan?

All escrow officers have war stories—stories we like to share—and you will find many of them as we go along whenever you see this icon 💣. These are real problems and issues we have encountered on the front lines (also known as the escrow officer's desk) and these symbols are put in here to emphasize what can happen.

💣 *After I completed a transaction on one condominium unit, I was informed that the buyer had ended up with the incorrect unit. The buyer wanted unit 105. He ended up with unit 110. Apparently, unit 105 was located on the southwest corner; unit 110 was on the northeast corner, and the developer of the complex did not label the door numbers to follow the same pattern as the legal numbers on the condo plan. It was a mad scramble a year after the fact to correct the legal ownership of units 105 and 110, as well as the documentation from both lenders. We only found out when unit 105 started a refinance process.*

CORRECT CITY

The location of the property in one city or another can make a big difference, not only for services that the buyer can expect, and the school district for children, but also to determine whether special transfer of ownership taxes apply, and whether there is a need for the city to send an inspector out as part of the local ordinance.

💣 *The City of Los Angeles encompasses a huge area, all the way from East Los Angeles to the San Fernando Valley. There are pockets within that area that belong to Los Angeles County and not the city, and there are other pockets that are their own cities, such as the city of West Hollywood. If the property is within the*

City of Los Angeles, the seller needs to obtain a residential property report and complete all its retrofitting requirements before the transaction is allowed to close. In addition, the City of Los Angeles charges an additional transfer tax of $4.50 per $1,000 of the sales price. In one case we handled, the costs that the seller had to pay increased considerably when we advised him of the extra requirements. Instead of getting some net proceeds back, the seller had to bring in funds to close escrow!

CORRECT SELLER'S NAME, ADDRESS, AND PHONE NUMBER

Obviously, providing a good address and phone number makes the settlement agent's job easier. Sooner or later we will have to call the client on the phone. But the seller's name, well, surprisingly, that may not be as simple or straightforward.

💣 *Same-name situation. We were informed that the sellers' names were Joseph Lidano and Maria Lidano and the title search report confirmed the names. Everything went on merrily until the sellers came in to sign the final grant deed, which had to be notarized. It was at that point, when we looked at the picture identification of one of the sellers that we realized the Joseph Lidano, who signed all of the paperwork, was not our actual seller. The original Joseph Lidano had passed away, and his son was actually Joseph Lidano II. Since his father had passed away, he didn't feel the need to use or sign with the II behind his own name any more. The son didn't mean to forge his father's name, nor did he mean to commit fraud, but there would have been serious repercussions if we had not caught the mistake. Joseph Lidano the Second did not have the right to sign for his father, even though the latter had passed away.*

* *Minors. About ten years ago I opened an escrow for a Ben Johnson on behalf of his son Michael (this was a refinance transaction, but the issue still applies). Two weeks into the transaction I was told by the loan officer that this was a no-can-do situation. Apparently, Ben was handling the paperwork because Michael was only eight years old. Ben thought that because he was the father, and he had custody of his son, he was able to represent him in all aspects, including signing for him. I hated to disillusion him, but even though he had full custody, he had to apply to the courts to be appointed his son's guardian in order to execute legal documents on behalf of his son, a minor (under eighteen years of age). The law allows a minor to receive and hold title to property so when the parents divorced, there was no problem when the mother gifted her share of the property to her son. However that was as far as it could go until the boy turned eighteen.*

CORRECT BUYER'S NAME, VESTING, AND CONTACT INFORMATION

Again, good contact information is essential, but more important is the buyer's full name and how he will vest his title, which is a science all of its own. We ask that the buyers give us their *exact* names, and they must match the names on their picture identification cards, especially if a marriage recently took place. After all, lenders will be drawing documents based on the names provided, and when signing these documents, the notary will need to see identification that matches. If anything is different, the notary may have a hard time fulfilling her obligation.

We often have foreign buyers with names that do not instantly identify whether the buyers are men or women, let alone if they are married or unmarried. These are things that are important to know at the beginning, and the information is not always provided. It is embarrassing when we prepare the documents and a single man becomes a single woman.

Tip: Whether you are a buyer or a seller, always, always check your name on the escrow paperwork right at the beginning. If it is incorrect, alert the settlement agent immediately to request a correction. Don't let it go until the very end.

💣 *When opening the transaction, the Martinez couple (Chapter Two, "It's All about Trust" section) gave their names incorrectly on the contract as "Elias and Anna Martines." The mistake, substituting an "s" for a "z," was never caught throughout the transaction until one week before the closing, when they came to sign their loan documents, at which time they pointed out the misspelling. In addition, Anna had never gotten her driver's license changed, so her driver's license still showed her maiden name of "Selena Anna Rodriguez." The loan documents all had to be redrawn and Anna had to find some other type of picture identification to substantiate her identity. The transaction was delayed for more than a week, and their lender charged the Martinezes an additional fee of $250 for redrawing the documents.*

Title and vesting: There are many ways to take title that may translate into tax consequences upon divorce or death. California is a community property state, so if you are married, the way you take title may make a difference in your future. Here is a general breakdown of the various forms of title:

- Individual
- Trust
- Corporation
- Limited liability company (LLC)
- Limited or general partnership (LP, GP)

Settlement agents are not allowed to give financial or legal counsel as to which type of title would be the best for a particular client. It is important that clients obtain their own independent counsel, preferably before the transaction is opened (see Chapter 3), especially if they have not yet set up their trust, corporation, LLC, LP, or GP.

There are also differences for an individual, whether single or married. Please refer to Appendices D-1 and D-2—vesting charts—at the back of this book.

Again, the importance of having all of the information—name, title, and vesting—right at the beginning of the transaction cannot be overstated. It could cause problems or delay the transaction if given incorrectly.

Tip: Before a decision is made, be sure you talk to your loan officer to make sure the way you take title will not complicate your loan application process.

❧ *Mr. and Mrs. Xavier Lin were purchasing a small apartment building with cash and no loan on a sixty-day time limit. The transaction was opened with their vesting to be determined. Two weeks into the transaction, their CPA recommended that they set up a corporation to buy this property. It took another two weeks for this corporation to be set up. All of the paperwork was corrected to show the corporation name. Then, forty-five days into the transaction and two weeks before closing, Mr. and Mrs. Lin decided they needed to get a loan. Upon contacting their loan officer, they were informed that getting a loan approved under their brand-new corporation was going to be almost impossible. So after all this time they had to rethink how to purchase the property, and the decision was made to use their trust. Now the trust had to be approved by the lender underwriter, further delaying the loan process. So a sixty-day escrow turned into a ninety-day escrow, and an all-cash transaction turned into one with a loan, resulting in a seller who was very, very unhappy and vigorously brought up breach-of-contract threats.*

For your benefit, here is a check list of other items of information needed at the opening table:

- Is there a preference as to which title company is used? Have you ordered a preliminary search report already with a particular company?
- Is a loan officer already assigned?
- Is there a homeowner association that we need to contact immediately to get documents for the buyer's review?
- Does the city in question need a residential property/ occupancy report?
- Does the transaction depend on either the seller or the buyer buying or selling their present property?
- Is the property considered income property for the seller, and will he or she be looking to do a tax-deferred exchange?

JUST HOW DO WE SPEND OUR TIME?

Once the purchase agreement has been signed, the time starts ticking. Tick tock, tick tock.

People have asked me if I can get a real property transaction closed in one week. Yes, I sure can, IF (and that's a very big if) the buyer comes in with all cash (no loan), AND the preliminary search report from the title company comes back clean.

The majority of transactions are a little more detailed, and after the trauma of the mortgage crisis in 2007, getting a loan has become a much more convoluted process. Lenders are requiring a full thirty days to process a loan from the beginning to the actual funding, and this is *if* the buyer is fully qualified and has clean records and high credit going into the transaction.

In my little corner of the country, contracts are normally written out for a *thirty-day* escrow (or sooner) time limit. This is not to say that the transaction cannot close sooner or later than that, but it is a *guideline* that everyone—buyer, seller, real estate agent, settlement agent, loan officer—works with.

Tip: If the parties involved remember that the transaction time period is not set in stone, and that there are many outside forces beyond our control, they will be less stressed.

A *forty-five-day* transaction always gives a little breathing room, but we understand that there are times when the transaction needs to be wrapped up quickly for one reason or another.

For a general timeline guide based on a thirty-day transaction, see Appendix B.

All good settlement agents will calendar the events that need to be watched and worked on once the file is opened. It's a matter of  organization as well as preservation of sanity. A popular escrow officer may have thirty on-going files on the desk at any given time. That is a lot to keep track of, and calendaring is a necessity.

Years ago, before sending documents via the Internet and wiring funds through the Federal Reserve became the norm, documents were shipped from coast to coast via Federal Express. During one particularly bad snowstorm in 1994, air freight came to a standstill for days. Documents were not delivered, and cashier's checks sent by customers could not get to us in time for closing. Here we were in sunny California, and yet a snowstorm back East had brought us to our knees.

Like all insurance policy exclusions, acts of God, terrorism and war are not covered.

MONEY MAKES THE WORLD GO ROUND

There is no doubt that right from the beginning, the closing costs (settlement costs) that go into the purchase/sale of a home are of the utmost concern for all parties, particularly when everyone's finances are tight. Every dollar counts! Surprisingly, depending on whether you are in southern California or northern California, the standard of who pays which costs can differ considerably and lots of dollars come into play. For example:

Main items of concern	Based on $500,000 price	Southern California	Northern California
Escrow Fee	$2,400.00	each pay 50/50	buyer
Owners policy title insurance	$1,832.00	seller	buyer
County transfer tax	$550.00	seller	seller
City transfer tax	$2,250*/ $3,400**	seller	each pay 50/50

*LA City
**San Francisco
Only certain cities have a transfer tax, and costs vary considerably.

Not all closing costs are delineated here. Escrow fees vary from company to company. An owner's policy of title insurance also varies, as each title company has its own published rates. Granted, there are exceptions to the above standard of practice, and the counties that lie in the middle of the state may go one way or another. As a comparison, with all else being equal, a seller selling a property for $500,000 in the City of Los Angeles would end up paying $5,832, and the buyer, $1,200. If the property were in the City of San Francisco, the seller would pay $2,250, and the buyer, $5,932. The goal, then, is to sell in the north and buy in the south!

If there are this many differences just in the various regions of California, you can imagine how many differences there are throughout the country. The thing to remember is that whether you are purchasing or selling a property, you should get a breakdown of the closing costs early on, directly from the settlement agent you are planning to use, because the standard is that there really is no standard. There are certain costs that have to be paid—that is standard—but who pays and how much is always a little bit different.

Here is a check list of some of the basic fees you will encounter. If your settlement agent doesn't have all of the answers, ask the responsible party for them:

- Settlement services fees—the basic fee plus all of the other incidentals that can be added on
- Title insurance premium fees
- Title insurance company incidental fees
- Government recording fees
- County transfer taxes
- City transfer taxes
- New loan charges, including:
  □ Appraisal
  □ Credit report
  □ Loan origination
  □ Processing and underwriting
  □ Prepaid interest
  □ Impound accounts for taxes and insurance
- Payoff lender charges, including:
  □ Principal
  □ Unpaid interest
  □ Document fees
- Termite and other repair costs
- One-year home-protection warranty cost
- Fire/liability/homeowner policy premium for one year
- City residential report fees
- Homeowner association fees
  □ Document fees
  □ Transfer fee

     ▫ Monthly dues
- Commission fees to real estate broker
- Property taxes proration and/or payment

Tip: Looking for a generalization of costs? For a buyer, figure 1 percent of the sales price. For a seller, figure 1 percent of the sales price. Then add on the percentage of the commission to be paid.

THE "OH-NO!" SECTION, OR WHY IT CAN SOMETIMES BECOME A FIGHT

Like anything else, there are certain things that a buyer, seller, or real estate agent *should not* do when something of this magnitude, involving so much money and effort, is being contemplated.

But before we begin the "Oh-no!" list, let me reiterate—*communication, communication, communication!* That is the absolute key to a smooth transaction. Look at it as if it is a car. If everything is running smoothly and every part does its job; it runs. If not, if one part does not interact properly with another, there is a breakdown. The magic words: communication and information flow!

FORGETTING TO TURN IN YOUR ESCROW PAPERWORK, OR TURNING IT IN LATE

Turning in paperwork in a timely manner allows the escrow officer sufficient time to check and make sure everything is filled out correctly and there are no issues such as alterations to the instructions (red flag!), or signatures not matching the typed names. This is also the time at which escrow officers will check to see if there is a similar-name situation that might affect the clients.

💣 *A seller turned in one piece of escrow paperwork—called a statement of information— the day before the closing. This form requires the seller to fill out his full name, Social Security number, driver's license number, and other pieces of personal information. It turns out that there was a lien against him personally for $1 million, which he claimed he was not aware of (a story that was hard for us to swallow), and perhaps he thought we would not notice if he turned in that form at the last moment. The transaction cancelled at the eleventh hour because of this lien and we had one upset buyer on our hands.*

💣 *In another case, our buyer inserted a handwritten statement above his signature line on our escrow instructions, stating "seller to have the foundation of the house inspected and repaired." These eleven words caused major issues and resulted in protracted arguments and recriminations between the parties involved. The file cancelled in the end.*

OFF ON VACATION

We all schedule our vacations in advance and sometimes this conflicts with what needs to happen in a transaction. For instance, is your vacation scheduled during the fourth week in the transaction when everything is happening all at once? If you can, avoid scheduling vacations during crucial periods. However, if the trip has been planned and there is no getting around it, let your settlement agent know as soon as the transaction starts so that alternatives can be planned. This applies not only to the seller and buyer but also to other parties who may be indirectly related to the transaction.

In another case it wasn't a seller or a buyer going on vacation but a third-party private lender of the seller's payoff loan. He took his family to visit relatives in Mexico in the middle of the sale. Unfortunately, he did not realize that his friend had sold the property on which his loan was secured, and we needed him to provide us with loan payoff figures and sign release documents before the transaction could close! After repeated efforts to contact this private lender, the seller finally found out that he had gone to a provincial part of the country where access to the village was by dirt road only—no telephone access. Our transaction was delayed by two weeks until the lender came back to town.

How about the case in which our seller went off on a cruise? He did inform his real estate agent, but the word did not get passed on to the rest of us. We were ready to finalize the transaction and needed him to sign the deed (ownership transfer document). This document had to be signed either in front of a notary public in the United States or at an American Consulate in a foreign country.

My seller was nowhere to be found. Again, delays were due to poor planning and communication.

NO PROBLEM—I HAVE POWER OF ATTORNEY

Not in town to sign? A power of attorney, whereby you delegate your duties and responsibilities to a third party, can be used. However, you can't use just any form. It has to be a standard form acceptable to the escrow officer, the title company, and the buyer's lender.

❧ *Our buyer had to sign by power of attorney, and he executed the form and gave it to his sister. By the time the sister gave us the actual power of attorney for review, we found that not only was it more than two years old, which is not acceptable, it was also in a format that was not approved by the lender or the title insurance company. By then we were into our fourth week of the transaction. A brand-new power of attorney had to be e-mailed to our client, and he had to make an appointment at the American Consulate in China to sign it (that in itself took one week) and then send it back by express mail. Our transaction was delayed by two weeks. The buyer blamed us! It could have been prevented if the buyer had given us the document for review prior to his leaving the country.*

ONE OF THE SELLERS IS A FOREIGNER

The IRS and California's Franchise Tax Board have special laws regarding foreigners selling their property in the United States. The law requires that a percentage of the sales price has to be withheld by the escrow holder and sent to these government agencies at the closing as a prepayment of income tax on the profit of the sale. In order to do this, the foreign seller has to have a tax identification number issued by the IRS. Without all of this, the transaction cannot close. Furthermore, if the foreign seller's net proceeds are not sufficient to cover the withholding amounts, the seller has to deposit enough funds into the transaction to close it.

💣 *My seller was a foreigner who did not realize he had to prepay income taxes to the IRS and the State of California upon the sale of his property. He was willing to pay, but he did not have a tax identification number (TIN). In order to close the transaction and pay the taxes, he had to first apply for a TIN. The original transaction time called for a fifteen-day closing. That transaction could not close due to the seller's TIN issue and cancelled. So did the next one after that. Finally, two months and two cancelled transactions later, the seller got his TIN and we were able to close.*

ONE OF THE SELLERS PASSED AWAY IN A FOREIGN COUNTRY

If a person passes away in a foreign country, we have to obtain a copy of the death certificate to establish the death. This certificate must be certified and accepted by the county recorder's office, and if it was issued by a foreign entity, the document first has to be translated by a court-approved translator (even if the document is mostly in English) and then certified by the county clerk's office before the county recorder's office will accept it for use. This is definitely an oh-no! situation if it is not handled properly early in the transaction.

DECLARING BANKRUPTCY

Declaring bankruptcy during a transaction means that all of the assets of a person are transferred to the jurisdiction of the bankruptcy trustee. This bankruptcy trustee then becomes the seller and will have to approve the sale. Filing bankruptcy is a common way of forestalling a foreclosure. However, if the seller is in a sale transaction when the bankruptcy is declared, this action will effectively stop the whole transaction.

DID I TELL YOU I AM GETTING DIVORCED?

It is already difficult to handle buyers and sellers who have divergent views of the transaction. Add to the mix two different sellers in the middle of a nasty divorce, and the whole file can become problematic. This is when our escrow fee may increase to take into account a lot of "he-said-she-said" calls, dealing with each party's attorney and general hand holding, not to mention arguments on how the seller's net proceeds have to be divvied up.

OH, THAT LOAN WAS PAID OFF AGES AGO

Settlement agents review the preliminary search report when they receive it and if the report shows an individual (not an institutional lender) holding a loan on the property, our antennae go up as they do on little alien figures from Mars. We immediately request that the seller get in touch with the individual lender to obtain the correct documents in order to release the loan. Too often the loan was paid off a long time before, but the correct release documents were never provided. Too often the individual has disappeared or even passed away. Too often it becomes a matter of a frustrated seller looking through old papers for anything relevant, or of us doing investigative work to find this private lender by all means possible.

☛* *My seller Jim inherited the property from his father, John. When John bought the property in 1964 he borrowed $12,000 from his seller, Robert. John had long since passed away and his son Jim had no idea that there was this outstanding loan on the property. We tried to find Robert through the general index for all of the counties in southern California and even tried to Google him, to no avail. Then we tried to find the third party on the promissory note—the trustee company—whose function it is to issue the release documents. We found out that not only was the trustee company defunct, the corporate officer had died also. All three players in this small private loan were no longer in existence. Finally, due to the age of the loan (forty-eight years!), we were able to convince the insuring title company to set the loan aside and issue a policy of title insurance overriding it. The whole process took weeks, but because it was caught early, it did not delay the transaction.*

LOCKING THE NEW LOAN INTEREST RATE TOO EARLY

I mentioned that in these tough economic times getting qualified for a loan takes a long time and lots of effort. However, as interest rates have fallen to all-time lows, impatient buyers may lock in their interest rates too early and for too short a period of time, thereby falling short of the closing period. For instance, if your 3.5 percent interest rate is good for only two weeks, don't lock the rate in until two weeks before the closing date. But what happens if you must lock in the low rate or lose it to a higher rate? Well, this would be a good time to negotiate with the seller for an earlier closing date if possible.

MY FUNDS ARE IN STOCKS OR A STOCKBROKER ACCOUNT

Settlement agents do not take personal checks to close a transaction. Stockbroker account checks are, simply put, personal checks. If you must sell your stocks for your down payment, do so far in advance of the closing date and transfer the funds into your regular checking account before you send it to your settlement agent. Remember that this process could take seven business days. Check with your stockbroker immediately upon the opening of escrow. Also remember that settlement agents prefer final funds to be deposited by wire, or at least by cashier's check, a few days before the scheduled funding date of the loan.

Tip: The buyer's lender wants to see a receipt for the deposit of final funds before they will fund the loan to the settlement agent. If the lender's funding cut-off time is 11:00 am, that means the escrow officer has to send a copy of the receipt of funds no later than 11:00 am. Be sure your funds arrive before that time!

MY FUNDS ARE COMING FROM OVERSEAS

Foreign governments have different rules and regulations regarding remitting funds overseas. Although we have no problem receiving money from overseas, foreign governments may have issues with allowing the funds out of their country. As a buyer, you should be aware of the different rules, regulations, and limits on sending money overseas. Some countries will allow an individual to send out only

$50,000 per year. Be sure this is checked far in advance to prevent any last-minute issues.

WHAT DO YOU MEAN I HAVE A JUDGMENT AGAINST ME?

In California, a lien or judgment against a person is like a computer virus. Once the lien or judgment is filed and recorded in the general index at the county recorder's office, it attaches to all of the real estate the person owns currently and might own in the future until it is paid, resolved, and/or released. A similar-name scenario is very common, especially if you have a common name, such as John Smith. It is important that the buyer and the seller turn in their escrow paperwork early so that we can determine if there are other liens or judgments that might affect them. If there are, the parties will need sufficient time to resolve the issues.

&ஃ *Remember Mr. James Kessinger? He did not realize that two other liens had been filed against his name in a defunct partnership several years before. He could have either negotiated with the creditor on an amount to pay, or he could have agreed to pay in full, no questions asked. Either way, the judgment had to be taken care of either by payment through the transaction or a release given to the settlement agent before the escrow could close.*

I WON'T DO REPAIR WORK UNTIL I MOVE OUT

Repair work to the property is normally done prior to the closing so that when the buyer does his final walk-through, he will also inspect the repair work done. It is important that the seller has a

THE ART OF ESCROW

good understanding of this, particularly if the repair work requires the seller to vacate the premises for a certain period of time (as in termite fumigation work). Often, sellers are loathe to move out until they actually have to give possession to the buyer. Sellers also do not want to incur the repair cost until they are sure the transaction will go through. How to balance the seller's wants and "musts" requires the real estate agent, or the parties involved, to communicate and negotiate if necessary. Problems caught in advance are much more readily solved than those that are left to the end when the pressure of time becomes the main concern.

I AM NOT READY TO MOVE YET, SO CAN I HAVE A FEW MORE DAYS?

Easier said than done! There are a couple of factors right off that have to be considered: (1) Is the buyer's loan going to expire in those few days? (2) Does the buyer need to move in because he has nowhere else to go? Again, this may not be a deal breaker, but these scenarios certainly call for tense moments that we can do without.

WHAT DO YOU MEAN MY ESCROW HAS NOT CLOSED? THE MOVING TRUCK IS PARKED ON THE STREET!

This one I have heard many a time, not only from the seller, but also the buyer, and it has everything to do with expectations and communications. I mentioned in previous sections that closing time periods are not set in stone. The parties have to realize that they shouldn't lock in the movers until they are certain about the closing date. At the opening of a transaction a savvy real estate agent or seller will ask that possession of the property be handed over to the buyer a few days after the closing date. This will give the seller leeway. On the buyer's side, don't give up your rental or previous home until you are assured of the possession date of your new home.

5

The Actual Process

CHAPTER FIVE

The Actual Process

JUGGLING

In the back of the book you will see Appendix B, which is labeled, "Life of an Escrow." This is a simple synopsis of the responsibilities of each party within the time frame of a transaction. Once the real estate agents have the offer and all counteroffers signed by both the buyer and seller, they take it to escrow so that escrow can be "opened" and life can be breathed into the file.

Upon opening:

1. The first thing that happens is that escrow instructions—the "map" of the transaction—are drawn up together with other paperwork for signature. Here is a check list that we in southern California normally prepare for buyers and sellers:
   □ Escrow instructions
   □ Commission instructions (if any)
   □ Seller's information form for payoff of loans
   □ Seller's confidential statement of information form (SS#, driver's license, birth date, ten-year residence history, ten-year work history, past marriages)

- Seller's Foreign Investment in Property Act form (FIRPTA)
- Seller's State of California Withholding Certificate form 593C
- Seller's 1099
- Trust certification (if title is under trust)
- Grant deed (ownership transfer document)
- Corporate entity documents if seller is a corporate entity
- Buyer's information form for loan and insurance
- Buyer's confidential statement of information form (SS#, driver's license, birth date, ten-year residence history, ten-year work history, past marriages)
- County-required preliminary change of ownership form
- Trust certification if taking title under trust
- Corporate entity documents if taking title under a corporate entity

2. Immediately upon opening, the escrow officer calls the designated title company to start a property search and issue a preliminary search report (also known as "prelim").

3. Unless there are a lot of ownership issues that require time to research, the prelim should arrive in a few days. It is extremely important that the settlement agent reviews the prelim immediately and carefully for discrepancies and unusual issues. The prelim is sent to the buyer to review, and copies get sent to the real estate agents.

Tip: The buyer should review the prelim carefully, especially if he or she is thinking of making future expansions to the property. Restrictions to building and expansion may show on the prelim.

4. Are there homeowners associations? Sometimes there is more than one! Hopefully, the seller has provided all of the contact information, as the settlement agent must immediately contact the association(s) for documents. As stated in previous chapters, the association has important documents regarding the ownership and management of the property—covenants, conditions, and restrictions (CCRs); by-laws; financials and budgets; rules and regulations; and board minutes—which may contain restrictions that could be a problem for the potential buyer. Other conditions might also deter a lender from lending money.

❧ *Two weeks into a transaction, we received the association documents for the buyer to review. It was a good thing that the buyer reviewed the documents carefully, because he found out that no pets over a certain size were allowed. His German shepherd exceeded the allowed size and the transaction cancelled. The seller was careful to disclose this fact immediately when the next offer was submitted.*

❧ *We had a transaction for the sale of one unit in a six-unit condo complex. Three of the units were not owner occupied, which meant that the condo complex did not meet Fannie Mae loan guidelines. The only way a loan could have been obtained was through a lender who would not sell it on the secondary market.*

Tip: Homeowner associations and/or the management companies that are employed to manage the association may require an upfront fee in order to release any information or paperwork. In order to save time and expedite the process, we usually give advance notice to sellers and their agents that they need to remit a check. If there is more than one association, the upfront fees can really add up.

During the first two weeks:

5. Contact the loan officer. With today's stringent underwriting guidelines, it is important that close communication be kept. The loan officer will immediately need an estimate of closing costs from the settlement agent in order to provide initial disclosures to the buyer within a certain period of time.

6. How many loans appear on the prelim against the property? Are there other liens or judgments that affect the seller? The settlement agent has to order payoff statements for all of these liens at least two weeks before closing in order to give sellers an idea of the amount of net proceeds they will get.

7. It's easy to obtain a payoff statement from an institutional lender but much harder from private lenders. If there are private lenders involved, we have to contact them early in the process so they can locate the correct documents and sign the required forms.

Tip: We urge sellers to call us before they makes their monthly mortgage payments so that we know whether or not we have to reorder a payoff statement to include the most recent payment.

Tip: Once the transaction is firmly in escrow and heading toward closing, we ask sellers to cancel any automatic monthly payment deductions from their checking accounts. Never rely on the lender to do it. The department that takes in the final payoff funds is never the same department that handles the automatic deductions. They may even be in different states, and you should never assume that they will communicate with each other regarding the status of your loan.

Two weeks prior to closing:

8. The settlement agent reviews the agreement and escrow instructions from time to time to see what is still needed to complete the file. Reminders are sent to the parties or their agents if certain required documents, information, or other conditions have not been received.

9. Normally, two weeks from the scheduled closing date, the seller, or his or her agent, will start worrying whether or not the buyer's new loan has been approved. Once approved, there is a great sense of relief for all. It's time for the settlement agent to review the whole file and figure estimated closing statements for both buyer (so he knows how much money to bring) and seller (so he knows how much he is receiving).

THE ART OF ESCROW

One week prior to closing:

10. The drawing of loan documents by the lender is the beginning of the end. If the lender requests the settlement agent to handle the signing, before calling the buyer in to sign, the settlement agent reviews the loan paperwork to make sure the following is reflected correctly by the lender: property address, buyer's name, and vesting. We also confirm with the buyer that the loan amount, interest rate, and terms are correct. If there are corrections to be made, it's better to let the lender know immediately, not when the buyer is sitting in front of us.

   Lender instructions that come with the loan package must also be reviewed and followed closely by the settlement agent, or the lender may not fund the loan. In addition, the lender may demand that the settlement agent bear certain responsibilities that are out of the settlement agent's control. Instructions like that are carefully reviewed by the settlement agent and the company's management to see if there will be future cause for concern.

💣 *We received instructions from one lender that stated that the loan packages had to be returned within forty-eight hours. If not, this lender might "assess a penalty of 1 percent of the loan amount plus any other fees incurred due to the late delivery of loan documents from settlement agents."*

11. Since lenders require that a property has fire and liability insurance coverage before they will fund a loan, the settlement agent makes sure the fire and liability insurance

chosen by the buyer is in place and a copy of the insurance document is included in the loan package.

12. Once the loan package is signed by the buyer and the proper documents are notarized, they are returned to the lender, together with any other documents that are required for the lender to review. Those could include insurance, a copy of the ownership grant deed, all instructions and amendments to instructions signed by the parties, and, most importantly, a copy of the buyer's and seller's estimated closing statements.

The lender reviews the package and alerts us if additional paperwork or corrections need to be made. This all takes time and normally a forty-eight-hour turnaround period is demanded by the lenders.

Tip: Lenders must review all of the paperwork in the transaction to ascertain that there are no issues that could be construed as defrauding the lender or others, rendering the loan unsalable on the secondary market.

13. Documents that have to be recorded at the county recorder's office are sent to the title company together with a copy of all of the payoff loans and liens that we have to pay on behalf of the seller.

14. Once the buyer sends in the final down payment, plus funds to cover all of the closing costs, we can request that the lender fund the loan.

An important notation must be made here. Although the buyer's down-payment funds are sent to the settlement agent, the lender's loan funds are sent to the title company. This is a fact that is not well known, but you can trace how the money flows in our Appendix C—"How the Cash Flows." Why are lender funds sent to the title company? The title company issues the final policy of title insurance to protect the lender's interest and with this responsibility the title company has to give written assurance that the funds it receives will be protected until the lender's loan is made of record and all previous liens and encumbrances are paid.

The day before:

15. The day that the lender funds the loan is called the "funding day," and on the West Coast this is usually the day before the closing or "settlement day." Unlike the rest of the states, California bases the settlement or closing day on the day that the deed and the mortgage documents are physically recorded or stamped and made of public record at the county recorder's office. It is important to note that for certain obvious reasons the lenders expect their mortgage documents to be recorded no later than the next business day after their funding date. They do not want their money sitting around without their mortgage documents being secured on the property.

16. When lenders fund the loan, they send us their funding figures—the loan amount minus all of their charges, plus any credits given. This net amount is wired to the title company, whereupon we alert them to this fact and we

"set up recording." In other words, we advise them that the moment has come to close the file. Together we go over the documents sent to them to be recorded; we instruct them what to pay off and what not to pay; and we let them know what types of policies we require for the buyer and for the lender.

17. With our call, the title company will "date down" the file, which means the company will do one final search to make sure nothing has been filed against the property or the seller since the last search. Remember that $1 million lien that the seller did not tell us about? That was found during date down. Escrow officers always fear receiving a phone call from their title officer at four in the afternoon before a closing. It's like getting a call in the middle of the night: it's never good news. Sometimes it is a call to tell us that the seller never paid his property taxes; sometimes it is a frantic call to tell us that someone filed a judgment against the seller a few days before; sometimes it is to tell us that one of the documents is not recordable because a signature was missing. Whatever the reason—and every escrow officer in the business has received calls like this—it is a mad scramble to see what can be done to rectify the situation. It's never a pretty sight. Sometimes the closing is delayed a few days; sometimes the correction can be done immediately, but always, always, it is a time of stress and tension for the escrow officer.

D-Day is closing day and what happens then will be picked up at the end of Chapter Five.

THE STRANGE CONCEPT OF TITLE INSURANCE

Unlike the ownership of a car or another object, ownership of real estate involves much more than ownership of the actual property. Ownership involves not only past and present rights and interest in the land, and the structure on it, but also  how that past affects future rights. There are also factors such as gas and mineral rights, subsurface rights, easements, and restrictions that affect the property and can be a totally confusing maze rarely understood by the consumer. It is a concern of the parties in a real estate transaction—seller, buyer, and lender—that the rights and interest in the property are clear and transferred correctly. So the purpose of title insurance is to insure that the past does not affect the future ownership of the property.

Unlike other types of insurance policies, such as health and auto, which are based on an assumption of risk, the assumption of risk in title insurance is minimized as much as possible before the policy is issued: the title company conducts a comprehensive search of the public records. All information pertaining to the property is gathered, from who the present owner is and what loans are secured on the property to what types of easements, rights of way, covenants, conditions, and restrictions exist from the time land records were made available. Also, the names of the present owner and the future owner (buyer) are searched in the general index records. As mentioned in other chapters, there are some personal liens that, once in the public record, attach to everything a person owns and become a lien against the real property also.

All of this is put together in a preliminary search report, which is the precursor to the final title policy report. This prelim is given to the settlement agent, who gives it to the buyer as part of his or her inspections and due diligence. The report will show the following:

- The name of the present owner of the property
- The legal description of the property, which is the location of the property on the county maps
- The address of the property as it shows on the county tax rolls
- The exclusions, or exceptions to the final title policy (items that will not be covered on the final title policy)
- The property taxes—present and delinquent
- Easements, covenants, conditions, restrictions, rights of way, and so on, that affect the property
- Liens, judgments, and loans that are secured on the property or that belong to the seller or that may show under the buyer's name

If there is anything unusual, you can be sure it will also be reported on the prelim.

☙ *We did a commercial property transaction in which the preliminary report showed an encroachment. One foot of the neighbor's structure encroached on our land. The seller had the right to demand that the neighbor remove that part of the structure. However, to do so would have meant that the neighbor would have to tear down the whole building. Therefore, an agreement was made. Our seller (with the approval of our buyer) would give the neighbor an easement, or the right to use of that one-foot strip of land.*

☙ *In another transaction the preliminary report showed that our seller did not have access to the street. He had owned the property for the previous thirty years, and, although he had no direct road access, he had been using a driveway that actually cut across his neighbor's lot, with the neighbor's implied consent. But there was never a right of way or an easement given for driveway purposes. It all came to the forefront during the sale, and our prelim showed this exception. In order to give clear title to the buyer, our seller had to go back to the neighbor to request a formal easement for access on his neighbor's land. Unfortunately, the original neighbor had passed away a couple of years before and the new neighbor did not want to grant this easement until he was given a sum of money in return.*

The cost for such a title policy is a one-time premium fee that is paid as part of the closing costs. The coverage is not renewed each year, as other types of insurance policies are. It is protection for the buyer's interest in the property as it is finalized *on the day of closing.* Protection may not be extended for any changes made afterwards by the buyer.

The settlement agent takes the preliminary report and goes through it, item by item, page by page, and notates everything that has to be cleared or paid, such as delinquent taxes and the seller's liens and judgments. If there are other exceptions that the buyer does not want to show at closing—for instance, the encroachment or the issue of not having street access—the parties have to work to get this cleared and removed from the prelim before closing. By the day of closing there should be a firm determination and understanding of what the policy will look like and what *exclusions* from insurance are agreed to. Unlike other types of insurance that list which coverages are included, the policy of title insurance lists what *will not* be covered.

So what is normally covered in a final title policy? Here is a basic list of the most important things:

- Impersonation of the owner
- Confusion arising from a similar name
- Forged deeds and releases
- Documents signed using a fake or expired power of attorney
- Deeds signed by minors
- Mistakes in the interpretation of a will or other legal documents
- Interest of surviving children omitted from a will
- Creditor claims against property sold by heirs
- Easements not discovered by a survey
- Community or marital property interests, or rights of a spouse still legally married
- Errors in tax records
- Documents claimed to have been executed under duress
- Claims by any other person to rights or liens on the property
- Losses sustained because of defects in the title due to past events

It is important to remember that problems may not be discovered until years later, and then claims can be filed that may be expensive to defend. As the title company picks up all of the expense of defense against these claims, to minimize the risk of such future claims, title insurance underwriting guidelines can be very strict. If certain things are claimed, like a loan was paid off, the title company may ask for proof much to the dismay (and sometimes anger) of the client.

There was a fraud case a few years ago in which someone refinanced a house time and time again within a matter of months by forging release documents with the help of fake notarial seals. The crook was able to con a number of financial institutions out of hundreds of thousands of dollars through several refinance transactions, all of which had title insurance issued. The forged releases came to light when the crook took off with the money and the lenders filed claims for forgery with the insuring title companies. This crook created quite a name for himself in the title industry. It is because title insurance underwriters are burned by cases such as this that make them very leery of accepting documents without substantive proof that the documents are not fake. Unfortunately, our law-abiding clients may not understand the reasoning behind the underwriting guidelines and feel that their honor and integrity are being questioned.

There are a number of types of policies that are commonly used in California.

- The basic standard coverage policy is the California Land Title Association (CLTA) Standard Coverage Policy
- The extended coverage policy is known as the American Land Title Association (ALTA) Owners Policy and Loan Policy
- The newest type of policy, only available for the owner-occupied single family home, is the ALTA Homeowners Policy.

The type of coverage for each is different and more coverage can be added. If there are certain unusual or different coverages required for a particular property—for instance, issues dealing with water rights or mechanic liens—added-on coverages, called endorsements, can be ordered at extra cost. It is the settlement agent's responsibility to order from the title company the right type of policy and the endorsements as requested by the buyer, and especially the lender.

BUYER'S RESPONSIBILITIES, PART ONE: DOING DUE DILIGENCE

I think I am one of the lucky people because about three months after I got started in this industry, I was given a small commercial property to handle. It was nothing major, just a little strip mall in the middle of a Los Angeles suburb called Eagle Rock. I had a commercial real estate broker who took pity on me and decided he was going to teach me some things and throw some large words at me. One of the things he talked about was due diligence, and later I found out that this was a term attorneys like to use. I use the term "due diligence" from time to time, and I want to make sure it is understood in the context of real estate transactions.

Due diligence is a very simple concept but very important when it comes to the purchase of real property. It means doing the necessary investigations of the property, whether they are physical inspections or inspections of books and records. Once the due diligence is done and approved, the buyer continues with the purchase.

For a purchase of a single family home, due diligence includes property inspections, usually by a licensed company, going to the city to inspect the permits, reviewing the preliminary report provided by the title company, and reviewing other disclosure and/or homeowner association reports that the seller provides. If there are questions or items of concern, this is the time to raise them. This is also the time when most negotiations happen, other than the original haggling over the price. If extensive repair is needed, or if there are issues such as the encroachments we discussed earlier, the buyer has to determine if he or she can live with the repairs the seller has agreed to do, and the seller has to determine if he or she is willing to do the repairs and at what cost. If either party disagrees, the transaction cancels. If the parties agree, everything proceeds as scheduled.

For a purchase of an income property, commercial property, or vacant land, due diligence is much more extensive, and the time period can be lengthy. It may call for the review of all of the tenant leases, income and expense reports, and even years of income tax returns. It may also involve going to the city or county agencies to review what they have on file regarding the property.

For the purchase of vacant land, the importance lies in not only reviewing a copy of the preliminary report but also all of the underlying documents—the documents that are public record. These underlying documents can be covenants, conditions and restrictions, easements, or rights of way, and may affect how and where the land can be developed. Going to the city's planning department is also important, and some buyers go so far as to draw up preliminary plans to build, and pass them through the planning department as part of their due diligence. Vacant land due-diligence periods are notoriously long, stretching from months to even a year.

In almost all contracts that I have seen, the buyer has a time period for doing his inspections and due diligence. Once that is done and satisfied, the transaction continues, and any funds deposited by the buyer to show good faith may become nonrefundable if the buyer decides to back out.

BUYER'S RESPONSIBILITIES, PART TWO: GETTING THAT LOAN

The second thing that the buyer is responsible for is getting his loan. I am not a loan officer and the intricacies of obtaining a loan are not my expertise and beyond the scope of this book. There are many books out there written by professionals in the financial industry, but in this book I want to devote a few words to how important it is for a buyer (or a borrower, if this is all about doing a refinance transaction) to scope out *early in the game* what type of a loan he will need and, more importantly, *what he will need to do or provide* to get it. In this section, my "buyer" can be interchangeable with "borrower," as the case may be.

We all know the standard loan to be 80 percent of the purchase price with a fixed interest rate and payments that are fully amortized of principal and interest over a thirty-year term. But there are other types of loans, and they run the whole spectrum, from this conventional loan to portfolio loans with interest based on the prime rate and due in one year or less. We also have loans, of which the seller is the lender, called "owner carry back loans."

With the exception of the owner carry back loans, the buyer needs to remember that any loan-qualifying process starts even before the property is found. Here are some pointers:

1. We covered enough of this in previous chapters, but be sure you look at your credit report and try to remove or eliminate the detrimentals. Does your spouse have lousy credit? You may want to leave his/her name off of the contract from the beginning.

2. Shop for a loan officer. Do you want a loan officer from a lending institution that can give you a direct loan? Or do you want a loan broker from a mortgage company that can shop the loans to various institutions to find the best rate for you? There are many lending institutions that grant their loans only through their own loan officers. Bank of America, Wells Fargo, and JP Morgan Chase are examples. You can't get a loan through them if you go through a loan broker.

Tip: First, always check with the loan officer of the bank where you have a checking or savings account. Use that as a starting point.

---

3. Make sure your source of down payment is ready and can be verified. The underwriter will check to see if this down payment has been in your account for a good period of time (at least three months). It's called "aging" your funds.

4. Are you getting funds from a relative? Be sure that your relative is ready to give supporting documents for these "gift funds" and let your loan officer know.

Tip: Please do not withdraw your funds from your account for any reason other than sending it to the settlement agent prior to the closing.

Tip: When you send any part of your deposit or down payment and closing funds to your settlement agent, be sure you send it from the banks that you listed on your loan application form and for which the lender has received a verification of deposit.

Our transaction started with husband and wife buyers. The deposit check came from the wife's account. However, it was determined later by the loan officer that she could not be a purchaser because of her bad credit. We had to cancel the transaction and return the deposit so that a new transaction could be opened under the husband's name only, and the new deposit would reflect funds coming from his account only. The wife had to quitclaim her interest in the transaction and ownership of the property.

In another transaction a buyer gave us his closing funds in three cashier's checks a few days before closing. After we sent a copy of the receipts and the checks to the lender, we were told that two of the cashier's checks had come from accounts that the buyer had not disclosed to the lender. We had to either return the two cashier's checks, which had already been deposited, or the whole loan file had to be resubmitted to underwriting for reapproval and verification of deposits from the other two accounts. It was a tough choice for the buyer to make. The buyer learned his lesson and more importantly so did we and the loan officer who handled the transaction!

5. Be sure you alert your employer that you are applying for a loan and that a verification of employment will be requested. Do not decide to change jobs halfway through this process. And if you lose your job right before the closing—well, we had that happen in one of our transactions. That was not a good day. Please note that right before the lender funds the loan, they will call your place of employment to verify that you are still employed there.

6. If you are self-employed or most of your income comes from a business in which no W-2 can be given, keep all of your bank statements and your income tax returns, because they definitely will be needed. If you have rental properties, be sure you have copies of your tenant rental agreements. In a nutshell, you will need to provide proof of your source of income. There are almost no more "stated income" loans in which you state what your income is on the loan application and the lender takes your word for it.

Tip: If you happen to be applying for a loan during the time when income taxes are due (January through April 15), either have your tax returns done early or show the lender a copy of your extension.

SELLER'S/BORROWER'S RESPONSIBILITIES

Whether this is a transaction in which we are looking to transfer ownership of the property to the buyer free and clear of all seller's liens, or this is a refinance in which the owner of the property is trying to qualify for a new loan, the most important responsibility of the seller/borrower (in this section I will use "seller" interchangeable with "borrower") is to provide us with the correct information on all of the loans that need to be paid off. And the earlier that is done, the better. We want no eleventh hour surprises to delay our closings. What do we need?

1. Correct name of financial institution and loan number. This may sound obvious, but it really isn't, especially in this day and age when loans are packaged and sold on the secondary market, not only once, but twice or more through the lifetime of the loan. You may start out with a loan from ABC Financial Bank and end up with XYZ at the end, going through the whole alphabet in between. Loans are being packaged and sold daily, and if your loan is in one of the packages, the minute you receive notification that your loan will now be sold and you need to start making your payments to XYZ, please let your settlement agent know.

🔥 *We had a transaction in which the loan was sold one week before the closing date. We had previously obtained a payoff statement but were in the middle of requesting an updated set of figures when the original lender told us the loan had just been sold. When we asked whom the loan had been sold to and requested further information, the lender was unable to give it to us due to privacy issues. The lender asked us to call the seller directly, because written notification had been sent. The seller had not received the letter, but we put him on notice. The minute the seller got the letter, he advised us. Unfortunately, when we called the new lending institution for an updated payoff figure, the lending officer was unable to give one to us. Apparently, although the loan had been sold to that institution, the staff had not had a chance to enter the loan into their system, and it would take two whole weeks for that process to finalize. Meanwhile, my escrow had to close. The old lender refused to take the money since that institution no longer had the loan. The new lender refused to take the money since it wasn't on that lender's system yet. Our escrow sat in pending status, and we called the new lender daily until we received confirmation that the loan was uploaded to that institution's system.*

💣 *The same scenario occurred in another transaction, but the twist in this case was that the loan was already in default. Our transaction was a short sale and when we tried to get an extension of the short sale, we found that the loan servicing had been sold and someone new was handling the paperwork. All of the short sale paperwork had to be resubmitted and reapproved by the new loan servicer. This short sale transaction was already into its sixth month and had to be extended another thirty days to accommodate the new servicer. The buyer lost his loan commitment many, many times.*

2. When you, as the seller, receive a call from the settlement agent telling you another loan or judgment or lien shows on the preliminary report, don't yell at the settlement agent.

Work with her to find out what it is and how to resolve the issue. Many times old loans that were carried by a now-defunct lender or a private individual, such as a seller carry back, may not have been correctly released when the loan was paid off. If you record a document against a property, showing that you have borrowed money, it stands to reason that when that loan is paid in full, another document will be recorded to say that the loan has been paid and released. That is how it works, but it's rare that people remember that. The general public does not know and does not think to ask an escrow professional what to do about a release until years have passed and the parties are long gone.

Any information the seller can provide will make the job easier for everyone involved, as it is his or her responsibility to track the institution or individual down. Sometimes consumers think it is the escrow officer's responsibility, but they should remember that we are not the cause of the problem, and all we can do is provide helpful suggestions on what can be done to find this institution or individual, or if the institution or individual cannot be found, what further can be done.

Sometimes it is not a paid off loan that is the problem. It is an unknown lien or judgment. From my experience, the first reaction from the seller is outrage. "What? Who? How dare they file a judgment? This was cleared a long time ago." If the judgment really concerns the seller, and his name and personal information are on it, then it will be his responsibility to find a way to obtain a satisfaction or a release. Contacting the filing attorney to start negotiations is the best first step. Perhaps with the passage of time, the person who filed the lien will be willing to take a lesser amount and release the lien or judgment.

Tip: A conscientious settlement agent will not contact a judgment creditor or his attorney without giving the debtor seller an opportunity to contact them first. This is because experience shows that once a creditor realizes there is an escrow transaction pending, he uses the opportunity to get the maximum amount of money possible. If there is no mention of a sale transaction, the seller stands a better chance of negotiating for a lower amount. Be sure you keep your settlement agent apprised of what is going on every step of the way.

---

* *I had a seller who had a judgment of $7,500 against him. After many weeks of negotiating with the attorney, he finally got it whittled down to $5,000 after he admitted that he really did not have the funds to pay any more. He got a statement from the attorney saying that he was willing to take a lump sum of $5,000 and would give my client a release once he received the funds. The seller sent us this attorney's statement a few days before the closing. When we closed the transaction and sent the money to the attorney, he rejected the payment and would not give us a release, which jeopardized my buyer's clear title to the property. The attorney said that in his negotiations the seller had always emphasized that he did not have the funds to pay the higher amount. When the attorney saw that the check came from an escrow company, he realized that the seller had more money coming to him than he had disclosed, and refused payment. The attorney wanted the full $7,500 plus interest accrued and attorney fees. By this time, two weeks after the closing, the seller had already received his net proceeds and refused to give any of it back. In order to clear this* *lien for the buyer and issue a good title policy, the title company and we, the escrow company, agreed to share and pay the difference. There were no happy campers in that transaction, except perhaps the buyer, who was unaware of all of the drama behind the scenes.*

3. It is the seller's responsibility to disclose any known defects in the property or the title, whether it can or cannot be seen. For instance, do you know you have a foundation problem? Do you know your pool has a leak? Do you know of a dispute with your neighbor regarding the block wall? A seller could be held liable in the future after closing if these known problems were not originally disclosed during the transaction. It's all about disclosure, not only to the real estate agent and the buyer but also to your escrow officer. As the escrow officer who will request the final title policy and its coverages, we have to pass on such disclosures to the title company. Remember, there are certain things that the title company will defend against. If a claim is submitted, and it turns out proper disclosure was not made, the title company can claim that the policy of title insurance does not cover it.

4. It is the seller's responsibility to make sure that all of the necessary agreed-upon repairs are made in a workmanlike manner and *in a timely manner.* Buyers will normally do a walk-through inspection prior to the closing. A conscientious seller who wants the transaction to close smoothly will put himself in his buyer's shoes and not only

make sure the work is done by the time the buyer looks at it but also that it was done properly.

⬤* *The seller contracted with the termite company to get the termite repair work done. The required wood repair was done; the rotted wood around the window ledge was replaced. However, that was it. It was left unpainted, a sore point with the buyer when he did the last look-over. How much would it have cost the seller to slap some white paint around that window ledge? Ten bucks? Instead, it raised a whole commotion in which the buyer insisted on looking at all of the other repairs with a fine-toothed comb. Aggravation? There is no doubt. The real estate agents were ready to tear their hair out. At the end it became a matter of principle between the buyer and the seller.*

Did I mention that this is an *emotional* process?

5. It is the seller's responsibility to move out of the property by the agreed-upon time. This might seem obvious, but you would be surprised by what can happen in thirty days, fourteen days, seven days, and three days. You start out with all the best intentions, but things happen. I had a seller who found out he could not move out on the predetermined date because he had made the wrong appointment date with his movers. Unfortunately, the buyers had their movers ready and waiting at the curb because they had to vacate their apartment.

And then there was the seller who refused to move out until his net proceeds were deposited in his bank. The reason? He didn't have money to pay his movers. The transaction closed late in the afternoon, and we were unable to wire his funds until the next morning. But the contract he agreed to stated that possession was to be given to the buyer at 5:00 p.m. on the day of closing. Do you think we had a problem?

YOUR ESCROW IS CLOSED! OR THE BATTLE IS WON!

This is it! The phrase every single escrow officer/settlement agent loves to announce to her clients. It means the culmination of a long process and the completion of a contract. If this is a transaction in which we had an "Oh-no!" incident (Chapter Four) or a war-story experience, this closing would achieve even more of a sense of satisfaction (and relief) than others.

I mentioned in my "Juggling" section in Chapter Five that one day before "D-Day" the buyer will have already sent his final down payment to the settlement agent, and the lender will have funded the loan to the title company. All that we are waiting for on this day is news of the recording of deed and the mortgage document (deed of trust), at which time we can consider the escrow "closed."

Unlike the "round table closings" on the East Coast, in California there is no gathering of parties at the closing agent's office, or signing and handing over of money and documents all at the same time. Here, everything is done beforehand, so on the closing day it is just a matter of waiting for news that the documents have been recorded at the county recorder's office. This can happen anytime between the standard working hours of 8:00 am and 5:00 pm. Once it happens, we receive "confirmation" (see Appendix E, "The Crazy Language of Escrow") that it is a done deal. All that is left is for us to ascertain the fees and payoffs, balance the debits and credits, and issue the final settlement statements. Keys are usually handled by the real estate agents without our involvement.

Tip: Don't sit around waiting for the phone to ring! Confirmation of closing can be sent anytime between the working hours of 8 am and 5 pm. For a busy county such as Los Angeles, where thousands of documents may be recorded on any given day, it could be late in the afternoon before we receive notification, particularly if it is on a Friday, or the last day of the month, or the last day of the quarter, or all three!

D-Day Arrives! So after all of the drama and the hair tearing and the ulcers, D-Day might seem a bit of a letdown. No fireworks, no popping of champagne (at least not in our office), no running around hugging each other with tears of joy. What does happen in our office is that we do what our name description says we do: we settle the accounts. That calls for waiting around for final figures to be sent to us, going through the file and making sure everyone who should be paid has a check going out and that all of the i's are dotted and t's are crossed. After all, we don't want future audits to find our files lacking. But most of all we want to be sure that we have performed our fiduciary duties to the best of our abilities, and that everyone is satisfied.

After D-Day:

- As always, a story never ends at the end. There is always an epilogue and in an escrow transaction the epilogue is full of things that have to be done after the closing.
- When the title companies send us their final title policy, we review it for accuracy and send it to the buyer and the lender.
- If there are any refunds, due to overpayments on the payoffs, they are sent to the correct parties.
- If the buyer's lender finds that a correction needs to be made to the closing statement, we make it, because if it is not made, the loan cannot be sold on the secondary market.
- Every year between February and April we provide copies of closing statements to our clients who have lost theirs so that they can finish their income tax returns.
- Finally, we always make ourselves available, when needed, to answer questions regarding the transactions we have handled.

6

Other Types of Transactions

CHAPTER SIX

Other Types of Transactions

YOUR HOME, YOUR CASTLE, YOUR BANK: REFINANCE TRANSACTIONS

I call this section "Your Home, Your Castle, Your Bank" because that is how people look at their homes. The refinancing of a property is, simply put, the process of obtaining new financing on a property, whether to lower the interest rate on the existing loan, to borrow money for other uses, or a combination of both.

A refinance of a property does not have to pay off the existing loan; there may not even be one to pay off. A refinance can also be used to put on an additional—or second—loan, such as a home equity loan.

A refinance also does not have to come from a financial institution; it can come from a private lender. There are many people willing to lend their money and get a better return than the measly 0.12 percent interest per annum that banks are offering in a money market account, or playing the stock market where there might be no return at all.

If you are borrowing from a relative or a close friend, he may not require a preliminary report on the property, and may not even ask for a lender's policy of title insurance, as a financial institution would.

But that would be unwise. We always encourage lenders, especially private lenders, to go through the settlement process. We encourage them to obtain both a preliminary report and a policy of title insurance, because those documents will provide not only peace of mind but also the security of knowing what the collateral looks like. They should confirm to their satisfaction that what the borrower told them before the loan was given was correct. Did he say he has only one existing loan on the property and this would be the second loan? Did he say that he paid all his property taxes? Did he say that he had no judgments against him? All of this would come out in the preliminary report. As a private lender putting a chunk of money into someone else's property, you should be aware of what the property ownership looks like.

A refinance escrow is really supposed to be a simple, straightforward thing, but it can bring up a lot of the same problems that occur in a purchase transaction. The only difference is that there is one less party to deal with: there is no seller. But his role is now taken by the lender. If it is an institutional lender, all of the previously mentioned things to watch for would apply.

- First, figure out why you want to refinance, and ask yourself if this will be detrimental to your finances.
- Second, clean up your credit.
- Look for a mortgage or loan officer who will get you the best rates.
- Take a good look at your house. Clean it up before the appraiser gets out there.

- Do you have a settlement agent you want to use? If not, your loan officer will recommend one. Be sure you check his recommendation out, and check the settlement agent's charges before you agree to use him.

Once an escrow is opened, the settlement agent will proceed to:

1. Prepare loan escrow instructions—instructions that will instruct the settlement agent on what your "road map" in this transaction will be. These instructions will also go to your lender.

2. Ask the title company to start a search of the ownership and public records of the property and issuance of a preliminary report.

3. If there are loans to pay off, we will contact the existing lenders to request a payoff statement.

4. Keep in communication with your loan officer throughout the whole period.

5. If requested by the lender, receive the lender's final loan documents once the approval is finalized.

6. Arrange for these loan documents to be signed by you, the borrower, and provide an estimate of the settlement costs incurred.

7. Follow the lender's instructions on obtaining what the lender needs prior to closing, for instance, fire and liability insurance.

In addition,

8. Once lenders receive all of the signed document and funding conditions, they will fund the loan.

9. Once the title company has received all of the mortgage recording documents from the settlement agent and the final loan funds from the lender, the company will proceed to record the documents at the county recorder's office.

10. The title company will pay off the liens as per the payoff statements obtained by the settlement agent, and the balance of any funds remaining will be remitted to the settlement agent.

11. The settlement agent will "settle" the account by balancing the file, and issue the final settlement statement to show to the borrower and his new lender.

12. The loan transaction is now closed. What remains is for the title company to issue the required policy of title insurance as requested by the lender, which normally happens within two weeks of the closing date.

Simple and straightforward? It can be, especially if the borrower has refinanced not too long before. The process is still clear in his mind and perhaps there is not much change in his credit, employment, and ownership of the property. It is all a matter, then, of finding the right lender with the right terms and conditions.

Complications do arise when the borrower has not obtained a new loan in a long time and his credit report or ability to qualify for a new loan are questionable, particularly in these post-mortgage-meltdown days.

Other complications arise when the ownership records of the property have not been reviewed and/or cleaned up in a long time. If you have owned a property for more than ten or fifteen years, would you even think you needed to review your ownership records? Remember Mr. Kessinger and his failed business partnership?

In my culture, as it is in others with strong family ties, it is very common for parents to grant their properties to their children, or back again, or from one relative to another and then back again. This all creates havoc on the ownership of the property. As mentioned previously, judgments and liens that are filed against a person attach to him and to everything he owns like a virus. This infection cannot be eliminated just because he gets rid of the property. The virus still remains and can only be eradicated by going to the source and asking the source to eliminate it.

💣 *Jose Delgado was going through a bad spot about ten years ago and granted his property to his brother Diego, just in case he could not resolve his troubles with his creditors and they filed some sort of judgment against him. Luckily for Jose, his matters were resolved in time. But the property remained under Diego's name for two years until Diego granted the property back. In 2006, during the mortgage boom, Jose decided to refinance his home. When escrow was opened, surprise! In the two years that Diego owned the property he also got himself into some financial troubles. Two judgments filed against Diego by his creditors attached to everything he owned, including Jose's property, because Diego owned it at that time. Even though Diego had granted the property back to his brother (done without title insurance), it did not eradicate the judgments. Now, in order to do anything with the property, whether it would be to refinance or even sell it, the two judgments against Diego had to be resolved. Not a pretty picture. I am sure there were words between the brothers that we did not hear about.*

This is just one of many, many examples of what can happen when property ownership is transferred back and forth indiscriminately with no further thought or long-range planning. It can really foul up a nice, straightforward refinance transaction.

UNDERWATER AND SINKING FAST: SHORT SALE TRANSACTIONS

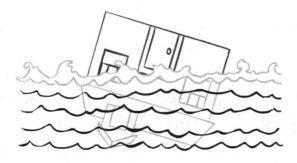

Ah! If a relatively simple and smooth standard sale transaction is like being dropped into Alice's Wonderland, a short sale is like taking a jump into Dante's Inferno because that is how bad it can get. The short sale is a standard sale or purchase of a property with a terrible twist.

The twist is that the seller is "upside down," or underwater, and he is hanging on by a thread. The amount that he owes on his property is more than the property is worth. The thread that he is hanging onto is his line to his lender, and this line is getting thinner by the day. Once it breaks, the lender will foreclose on the property and the property sinks. But if the thread is still there, there is always a chance that the seller may still sell the property for less than what his mortgage balance calls for, if his lender agrees. This is called a short sale.

The process is long, protracted, and at times out of our control:

1. The seller needs to agree to the process. This means he has to pull together all of his financials and submit all sorts of documentation proving that there are reasons he could not keep up with the payments. And they have to be good reasons. "Just because" is not a good reason.

2. You need a short sale negotiator or a real estate agent who is hungry enough and experienced enough to deal with the ins and outs of a short sale and willing to help the seller negotiate with the lenders.

3. You need a buyer who is not only willing to buy but willing to wait a long time for the process to finalize. That means the purchase price negotiated has to be a good incentive.

4. You need a sharp-enough escrow officer who can juggle the many deadlines and other obstacles and is willing to handle it for less than she would receive in a normal transaction.

5. And finally, you need a lender or lenders (there may be more than one, and what a juggling act that becomes!) who is/are willing to consider the short sale at the buyer's offer price and a loss mitigation specialist, who is probably overwhelmed with files, to carry it through.

If all of the above are in place, the steps are the same as they are in a standard purchase transaction, with just a few exceptions:

Before agreeing to the offer price and issuing a short sale approval letter, the lender will require the real estate agent to provide a broker's property opinion letter (BPO) showing the market value of the property. The lender will also need an estimated settlement statement from the escrow officer to show what net proceeds will be left after all of the other costs are paid. Those net proceeds will all be given to the short sale lender to apply toward the seller's unpaid loan balance(s).

This is where the escrow officer has to be very careful and very thorough because once the settlement statement is submitted and approved, changing any figures on it will require the whole package to be resubmitted and reapproved. What are some of the factors that can come into play?

- Unpaid property taxes
- Homeowner association transfer and document fees, unpaid dues, and hefty attorney fees if those dues have gone into collection

- Other liens and judgments against the seller that may have attached to the property (one of the first things an escrow officer will do is order the title search as soon as possible)
- Requests for credits to go back to a buyer to pay for closing costs
- Demands from a junior lien holder—the lender who is holding the junior mortgage
- Demands from the buyer's new lender regarding updating the condition of the property, especially if the new loan is a government-guaranteed FHA loan

In a short sale transaction it is not our seller who is in the driver's seat, it is the short sale lender(s), and in particular, the first lender. Any issues that might reduce the approved net proceeds figure need to be avoided. Buyers who seek to purchase under a short sale need to realize that they may not get what a seller in a standard transaction may be willing to pay: termite and other repair work, home protection policy, and credits toward their closing costs. In fact, the buyer may even have to pay for part of the seller's costs that the short sale lender will not allow to be deducted from the net proceeds.

When the short sale lender sends the short sale approval letter, they delineate in it everything that they have agreed to:

- The purchase price
- The names of the approved buyers (changing a buyer requires the whole package to be resubmitted)
- The minimum net proceeds they are willing to take
- The allowed real estate commission to be paid
- The allowed closing costs, sometimes itemized by type of cost
- Any other costs they are willing to see paid
- The approval expiration date

When an escrow officer gets the letter, the first step is to review it line by line, checking each item against the original estimate settlement statement. Any discrepancies have to be brought to the parties' attention. For instance, the letter may state that no payment of delinquent association dues is allowed, or that no tax prorations are allowed, or, heaven forbid, that the commission is reduced or the settlement agent's fee is reduced. If this happens, everyone gets involved in figuring out who needs to make up the difference.

The letter always has a final performance date, and irrespective of whether the actual contract calls for a later date, the lender's demanded date is the one to work by. As it is important for the escrow officer to make sure everything is in place for the closing on or before that date, it is important for the buyer to make sure he can get his new loan in place and ready to fund by that date. If not, an extension has to be requested, and not only does that takes time, the lender may request that extension penalties be added on.

Normally the property is already under foreclosure when a short sale is being contemplated. So it becomes very, very important for the escrow officer and the real estate agent negotiating the short sale to keep a sharp eye out for the foreclosure sale date, the date when the property goes to sale/auction. If the short sale has not closed by the foreclosure sale date, calls must be made to postpone the foreclosure sale date to give the short sale an opportunity to close. We have had a case in which the property was sold right from under us at auction while we were handling the short sale. Never, ever assume that the foreclosure department knows what the short sale department is doing with the same loan. They could be in totally different states, and they do not necessarily talk to each other.

What happens when there is more than one loan in a short sale? First of all, each short sale lender has to be approached with a request for approval and to submit its own short sale letter. The seller and his real estate agent have to negotiate with each lender individually and as a whole with the understanding that the first lender, who has the priority, is informed on what the second, or junior lenders, want. Normally, the first lender gets the bulk of the proceeds. The junior lenders get only the amounts that the first lender will allow to be paid, or they have to demand someone else pay the difference. When there is more than one short sale lender in a transaction, it becomes a juggling act because the demands of all of the lenders have to be satisfied so that the transaction can close on the earliest date demanded.

We had a transaction for the sale of a $500,000 home, in which there were three lenders with claims against the property. The first lender (ABC) had a loan with an unpaid balance of $400,000. The second lender (DEF) had a loan for $170,000. The third lender (XYZ) had a loan for $100,000. ABC was in great shape because even with the closing costs he would still get all of his money back. The short sale was thus conducted for DEF and XYZ. ABC's short sale letter showed that principal, unpaid interest, and attorney foreclosure fees added up to $450,000. This would leave only $50,000 to pay DEF and XYZ, the 6 percent commission, the closing costs of $2,200, and unpaid taxes of $6,000. DEF demanded $10,000, and XYZ demanded $10,000. The shortage was $8,200. After much posturing, the real estate agents agreed to reduce their commission to 5 percent and the buyer agreed to pay the balance. At least this case worked out "happily ever after."

In another case in which there were only two loans, the second lender requested a payoff of $12,000 and refused to budge *from this amount. The first lender would allow only $2,000 as payment to the second lender. No one—buyer, real estate agents— was willing to make up the $10,000 difference. After all of the time and effort spent on the transaction it cancelled when negotiations could not achieve the desired result.*

The single most important word for a short sale transaction is *patience,* and this goes for all parties involved. We all need patience because the control of a short sale is not in our hands. It is in the hands of the staff in the lender's loss mitigation department. To them, this file could be one of hundreds of similar files. They are really not invested in having a smooth and expeditious closing of our transaction. On this side of the negotiation table the process is handled by a real estate agent on behalf of the seller. This agent needs to be sharp, knowledgeable and able to see the whole picture at one time, especially when there is more than one short sale lender involved.

SUNK! OR LOSING THE FIGHT: THE REO TRANSACTION

If the seller has not paid his mortgage and there is no short sale attempt, or if the seller could not get a loan modification on the original loan, the property is foreclosed by the lender and it becomes an REO, or "real-estate-owned" property. Contrary to what you might hear on the street, lenders really would rather not foreclose if they can help it. It is time-consuming, it is resource-consuming and in the end lenders may not get as much for the property as they would in a short sale or even a loan modification. Foreclosure is really the last resort for most lenders.

On the sale date, when a property is auctioned off, there is a possibility that a consumer will come in with a winning bid and the lender can sell the property without having to worry about foreclosing. If no one bids, the property is deeded to the lender and it becomes an REO property, whereupon it goes through many channels before it is listed for sale.

The sale of an REO is like any other sale, except:

- The seller is a financial institution and contract approvals and the signing of paperwork might be handled through a designated third-party servicing agent. The asset manager makes the decisions, but he is purely behind the scenes and he has no direct contact with anyone except the real estate agent representing the REO seller

- Normally the REO seller will not pay for any repair work. Property is sold in as-is condition. What you see is what you get.

- Any changes to the contract, or extensions beyond the time period allowed by the REO seller, must be approved early on, and extensions may require penalties. Time is of the essence. Be ready to close as called for on the contract.

- The REO seller normally uses his own settlement agent and title company, relying on their established fee schedule, but if the buyer insists on using his own choice the buyer may be required to pay the seller's closing costs as charged by the buyer's company of choice.

- The REO seller may require certain deed restrictions, such as a statement that does not allow the sale or encumbering of the property for a certain period of time after closing. This is to prevent the practice of "flipping" the property.

- REO sellers prefer "all-cash" transactions, and those in which the buyer has done his due diligence prior to entering into the contract.

If you are contemplating the purchase of an REO property, remember to do your due diligence first and get a good sense of what will be needed to bring the property up to par. The property may be in very, very bad shape and require lots of work. The foreclosed owner may have torn up the house when he vacated, and if the property has stood empty for many months, vandals may have been in and out. The REO seller may do minimal repairs prior to putting the property on the market, but he normally won't negotiate for more to be done once the transaction is under contract. At that time he just wants to get the transaction closed and off his books, especially if it is nearing the end of a month or a quarter.

7

In Conclusion

CHAPTER SEVEN

In Conclusion

THE PROFESSIONAL

I started my story with Mr. Wyznovski and I would like to end with him. I will always remember Mr. Wyznovski very fondly, not just because he was the impetus for me to write this book but because as nervous as he was, he was willing to give a wet-behind-the-ears, newly minted escrow officer a chance at handling his transaction thirty-some years ago. He did not have to trust me. He could have gone to a more experienced escrow officer, but he gave me this chance, and because he did, he changed my whole life.

On this path I have encountered many types of people. I have experienced many interesting, sometimes exasperating, sometimes emotional stories, gone through the roller coaster of the economic cycles, and even had the very dubious experience of looking down the proverbial barrel of a rifle (lawsuits) a time or two.

After all of the Wyznovskis, Kessingers, Cheungs, Martinezes, Stewarts, and Lins, one common thread runs through this book. A settlement agent is the *professional* you are looking for when you are in the process of selling, buying, or refinancing a home.

This is a person you can *trust,* who will keep your information and background *confidential,* who will be *impartial* to all, and will provide you with an *accounting* of every penny of your money spent.

Many of us are members of our professional industry organization, the California Escrow Association, or a member of the Escrow Institute of California, or both. And certainly, no matter which state you are doing business in, your settlement service professional should be a member of the national American Escrow Association.

Processing a transaction smoothly from beginning to end requires the buyer and the seller to be *prepared* and *organized,* and to do their share of presale/prepurchase work. At times, *patience* is required, but always *cooperation* and *communication* between these parties and the four professional industries in the equation: the real estate industry, the title industry, the mortgage industry, and the settlement services industry.

Processing a transaction requires providing the *right information* expeditiously (remember the old adage: "Garbage in, garbage out"?) and a whole lot of *common sense.* It is unfortunate that through the years the escrow process has been a real mystery. And because people tend to ignore that which they do not understand, we have become the invisible toilers who are forgotten when things conclude satisfactorily, but marched out first in line to meet the firing squad when things go badly.

We all know which professional you go to for different things in your everyday life, for instance:

A doctor when you are feeling ill;

A teacher to teach your child;

An attorney when you have a legal matter;

An accountant when you have a financial issue;

A loan officer when you need to get a loan;

A real estate agent when you need to sell or find a home.

And when you find the home to buy or you find the buyer for your home, you need to go to your professional settlement agent to complete the process.

This book is about the escrow process. Make no mistake. It can be a battle, and we who are in this business see ourselves as being at the front of the battle lines. We look forward to the point in the process when we can announce triumphantly, "Your escrow has closed!" Yes, it is a fight, but once it is fought and won, your American dream will become a reality. And that is our ultimate goal.

APPENDICES

Escrow, In the Center of Things

Life of an Escrow,
simplified timeline for 30 day time period

Time	Escrow	Buyer	Seller	Title	RE Broker	Lender
Acceptance		Sign contract	Sign Contract		Submit Contract to Escrow	
Week 1	Prepare documents. Order Title Search	Sign and return escrow paperwork. Application to Loan Officer. Do physical inspection	Sign and return escrow paperwork. Check out Termite inspections and repair work costs	Start property title search and issue preliminary report	Help clients with physical Inspection, termite inspections, repair work	Start loan process
Week 2 - 3	Review preliminary report. Order Seller payoff figures. Communicate and provide necessary documents to Lender	Review prelim. Continue loan application. Get insurance quotes	Make sure all repairs are made. Make arrangements to move	Send completed prelim report to Escrow	Follow up on repair work. Check on new loan status	Submit loan documentation for underwriter approval
Week 4	Figure Buyer, Seller closing estimates. Contact Buyer to sign loan docs. Order Buyer insurance, review all conditions of transaction are met. Send filing documents to Title Company	Buyer sign loan documents. Send downpayment to Escrow. Do final walk-through of property		Check all documents received. Date down file for closing	Do final walk through with Buyer	Send loan documents to Escrow
Day before closing	Work with Lender for last minute funding conditions. Is everything in? Set up closing.			Send documents - Deed, Mortage documents to County for recording		Send loan funds to Escrow/Title. Provide Escrow with final loan charges.
Closing date	Balance file with figures from Lender and from Title company. Generate final closing statements for everyone, including Lender. Cut checks to pay all Vendors, RE Brokers, net proceeds to Seller and refund to Buyer.	Move in? Depends on pre-agreed possession of property date	Move out? Depends on pre-agreed possession of property date	Payoff Seller loans and liens, send figures and balance of loan funds to Escrow	Arrange for delivery of keys from Seller to Buyer	
After Closing	Send policy of title insurance to Buyer			Issue Policy of Title Insurance - sent to Escrow and Lender		

How The Cash Flows

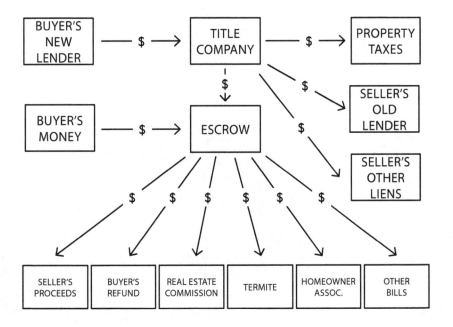

Vestings: How to Take Title to a Property

		STATUS	DESCRIPTION	VESTING TO USE
INDIVIDUAL OWNERSHIP	Sole Ownership	Single	Never married	A Single Man/Woman
			Divorced/ not married now	An Unmarried Man/Woman
			Spouse passed	A Widower/a Widow
				An Unmarried Man/Woman
		Married	Sole ownership (requires spouse Quitclaim)	Married Man/Woman as Sole & Separate Property
	Joint Ownership	Between Married Couples (See Chart D-2 for differences)	Husband and wife	as Joint Tenants
				as Community Property
				as Community Property with Right of Survivorship
		With Others (See Chart D-2 for differences)	(all together with right of survivorship)	as Joint Tenants
			Undivided ____ % interest (no right of survivorship)	as Tenants in Common

	ENTITY TYPE	SIGNATORIES	REQUIRED DOCUMENTS
CORPORATE ENTITY OWNERSHIP	Trust	Trustees	Trust Agreement, its Amendments & Trust Certification
	Corporation	2 Corporate Officers	Articles of Incorporation & Corporate Resolution
	Limited Liability Company (LLC)	Managing Members	LLC-1 and Operating Agreement
	General Partnership	All partners	Statement of Partnership & Partnership Agreement
	Limited Partnership	General Partners only	LP-1 & Partnership Agreement

Title can be taken in a combination of individual and corporate ownership
EXCEPTION: Individual ownership cannot be taken with Corporate Entity Ownership in "Joint Tenancy" mode.

The way to take title is a very personal matter. Parties are cautioned to check with own their independent financial and legal counsel to determine which way best suits their particular needs.

VESTING

METHODS OF HOLDING TITLE (INDIVIDUALS)**

	TENANCY IN COMMON	JOINT TENANCY	COMMUNITY PROPERTY	COMMUNITY PROPERTY with right of survivorship ("new")
Who can take title?	Any number of persons (can be husband & wife)	Any number of persons (can be husband & wife)	Only husband & wife	Only husband & wife
How is ownership divided?	Ownership can be divided into any number of interests, equal or unequal	Ownership interests must be equal and cannot be divided	Ownership interests are equal	Ownership interests are equal
Who holds title?	Each co-owner has a separate legal title to the individual's undivided interest in the whole property	There is only one title to the entire property	There is only one title to the entire property	There is only one title to the entire property
Who has possession?	Equal right of possession	Equal right of possession	Equal right of possession	Equal right of possession
How do owners convey their interests?	Each co-owner's interest may be conveyed separately by it's owner	Conveyance by one co-owner without the other breaks the joint tenancy and owners then become tenants in common	Both co-owners must join in conveyance of real property. Separate interest cannot be conveyed	A written declaration on the face of the transfer document, signed & initialed by the grantees. May be terminated in the same manner
What happens in case of death?	Upon co-owner's death, the interest passes by will to be decedent's devisees or heirs. No survivorship rights	Upon co-owners death, his/her interest ends and cannot be willed. Survivor(s) owns the property by survivorship	Upon co-owners death, it goes to survivor in severalty. It goes by will to decedent's devisee or by succession to survivor	Upon spouses death, title to the property will vest in the surviving spouse
What is successor's status?	Devisees or heirs become tenants in common	Last survivor(s) owns the property in severalty	If passing by will, tenancy in common between devisee & survivor results	Surviving spouse owns the property in severalty
What is creditor's interest?	Co-owner's interest may be sold on execution sale to satisfy a creditor. Creditor becomes a tenant in common.	Co-owner's interest may be sold on execution sale to satisfy creditor. Joint tenancy is broken. Creditor becomes tenant in common	Co-owner's interest cannot be seized and sold separately. The whole property may be sold to satisfy debts of surviving spouse	Co-owner's interest cannot be seized and sold separately. The whole property may be sold to satisfy debts of surviving spouse

** Parties are cautioned that they should obtain their own independent financial and legal counsel regarding how to take title.

Escrow Holder is not authorized to give legal or financial counsel.

The Crazy Language of Escrow

Escrow language can be very alien at times and in our excitement we forget that the person we are talking to may have gone through a transaction only once or twice in his lifetime. With the added language or cultural difference, sometimes what I am trying to convey to my clients may make absolutely no sense. Escrow has its own particular vernacular, made up of acronyms, synonyms, and short hand, at times quite different from the real estate terms used by professional real estate agents.

Here is a list of special terms that we use in California in our everyday escrow lingo. Next time you call me, and I ramble on about "pres" and "benes" and "zero demands," hopefully you will know exactly I am trying to say!

1099	IRS form issued by escrow to seller to report the sale of the transaction for income tax purposes.
9-A	City of Los Angeles 9-A Residential Property Report.
ADJUSTABLE	A type of loan in which the interest rate is not fixed.
AIR form	American industrial real estate/commercial real estate purchase contract form.
AITD	All-inclusive trust deed—a type of loan given by seller to buyer.

ALTA policy	American Land Title Association policy of title insurance. Usually means the policy insuring the new lender of a property.
APN	Assessor's parcel number—identification number assigned to each property by the county tax assessor.
APR	Annual percentage rate—loan term used to describe the annual interest rate.
ARMs	Adjustable rate mortgage—see "Adjustable."
BENE	Beneficiary—the person or entity who lent the money on the property; the lender.
BONA FIDE	Real, legitimate, in good faith and without fraud.
BPO	Broker price opinion letter—document provided by real estate broker showing the value of the property, for a short sale lender.
CAR contract	California Association of Realtors purchase contract form.
CC&Rs	Covenants, conditions, and restrictions setting out limitations and conditions of the property.
CDA	Commission disbursement authorization—authorization from real estate broker on how to disburse commission at closing.
CLOSED	The status of a file when all documents have been recorded, and ownership and the new loan are transferred.

COE	Close of escrow—the date of closing of transaction.
CONDO	Condominium—a property that is part of a unified development complex that has an association to manage the complex. Can be a home or commercial property.
CONFIRMED/ CONFIRMATION	Acknowledgement that all documents are recorded, and ownership and the new loan are transferred.
CPL	Closing protection letter—letter from title company to lender to acknowledge responsibility for loss incurred for failure to follow lender's instructions at closing.
DEED	The grand deed—the document that transfers the ownership of a property.
DEMAND	The document issued by a lienholder that states how much needs to be paid.
EASEMENT	A right or interest placed on the property to benefit someone else.
EDD	Employment development department— California government agency that handles employee/employer taxes.
EI	Escrow instructions.
ENCUMBRANCE	A debt or a claim against a property.
ENDORSEMENT	A document attached to the title or other insurance policy that adds to or subtracts from the standard insurance coverage.
EOI	Evidence of insurance—proof required by lender that there is or will be insurance on the property.

ESCROW ACCOUNT	Term used by lender, same as impound account—see "Impounds."
EXCEPTIONS	An item now existing on the property that the title company will not insure.
FANNIE MAE	Federal National Mortgage Association, aka FNMA—government-sponsored entity that provides money for loans to financial institutions.
FEE (title)	Type of ownership of property (as compared to "leasehold").
FHA	Federal Housing Administration— goverment agency under HUD, used to insure loans made by financial institutions.
FIRST	The first loan on the property.
FIXED	A type of loan in which interest does not change through the life of the loan.
FREDDIE MAC	Federal Home Loan Mortgage Corporation, aka FHLMC—government-sponsored enterprise that buys loans from financial institutions and sells them as mortgage-backed securities.
FTB	Franchise Tax Board—Californian govern-ment entity that collects personal and corporate income taxes.
FUNDING	The status of a loan in which the lender is ready to release the money that is being loaned.
GD	Grant deed—the document that transfers ownership.
GFE	Good faith estimate—required document provided by loan officer to disclose fees.

GRANTEE

The person who is receiving the property.

GRANTOR

The person who is selling or giving the property.

HECM
(pronounced as "hekem")

Home Equity Conversion Mortgage—reverse mortgage program administered by FHA.

HELOC

Home equity line of credit—A line of credit mortgage against property that borrower can draw upon and/or pay back at any time during the term.

HOA

Homeowners association—the group of owners who manage the condominium project.

HPP

Home protection policy, aka home warranty plan—insurance protection for building and fixtures.

HUD

The Department of Housing and Urban Development. Government agency that is responsible for housing market programs, such as FHA.

HUD-1

Nationwide, standardized, closing statement established by HUD to transmit fees and closing costs to buyers and sellers.

IMPOUNDS

Loan term used to describe amounts collected by lender for taxes and/ or insurance along with the monthly payments.

JT

Joint tenancy—type of vesting to hold title in real property.

JUDGMENT

A court-approved lien that is filed against a person who owes money.

JUNIOR (to)	A loan that is behind one or more loans that were recorded before it.
JURAT	The form used by notaries when notarizing a party who has to swear under oath.
L&V	Legal and vesting—a document that shows the present legal description and ownership of property.
LEGAL	Legal description—the location of the property on the county maps.
LIEN	A debt against a person or a property.
LLC	Limited liability company.
LP	Limited partnership.
MIP	Mortgage insurance premium—insurance required for FHA loans to offset any losses by lender if loan cannot be repaid.
MORTGAGE	The loan on the property.
NHD	Natural hazards disclosure report.
OA	Owners association—same as homeowners association, but for commercial properties.
OWNERS (policy)	Policy of title insurance that insures the new buyer's ownership of property.
PAYEE	The person who is getting paid.
PAYOR	The person who has to pay.
PCOR	Preliminary change of ownership form—to be attached to any transfer of ownership deed that is being recorded.

PD	Professional designation given to escrow people who have passed the tests given by the California Escrow Association.
PITI	Principal, interest, taxes, insurance—the main payments of a property owner.
PMI	Private mortgage insurance—insurance paid by borrower on non-FHA conventional loans to offset any losses by lender if loan cannot be repaid.
POA	Power of attorney.
POINTS	A fee charged by lender for the loan. One point equals 1 percent. Separate from any other fees.
PRE or PRELIM	Preliminary search report issued by the title company to show who owns the property, the liens, and the exceptions that won't be insured.
PREFIGS	Preliminary figures for costs and payoffs provided by title company before the actual closing.
PRIOR TO DOCS	Lender-required conditions that have to be met before loan documents can be issued.
PRIOR TO FUNDING	Lender-required conditions that have to be met before the loan can be funded.
PROBATE	Process of submitting to the court for approval of the sale of property in cases in which owner has passed away.
PRORATE/ PRORATION	Dividing charges between buyer and seller so that each pays his share based on the time of ownership of property.

PSA	Purchase and sale agreement.
PUD	Planned unit development—single family home that is part of a unified development that may have an association that manages the complex.
PULLED	When a recording did not go through because of a last-minute problem at the title company or at the county recorder's.
QUITCLAIM	The document used to transfer certain interests in the property—see our FAQ—or, as a verb, the act of giving up interest.
RECON	Reconveyance—release document used to show a loan is paid in full.
RECORD	The action of recording a document at the county recorder's offices to make it a public record.
REO	Real estate owned—properties foreclosed and now owned by financial institutions.
RELEASE(S)	The document used to show a lien is paid and no longer affects the property.
RESPA	Real Estate Settlement Procedures Act—passed by government to monitor lending and settlement practices against consumers.
RIDER	An attachment to a document, normally, an attachment to the deed of trust.
SBE	State Board of Equalization—California government entity that collects sales and other taxes.
SECOND	The second loan on the property.

SERVICER	Servicing agent—the institution that is collecting the payments for a loan on behalf of the actual lender.
SFR	Single family residence.
SI	Statement of information—a form to be completed by parties in escrow stating certain personal information.
SINGLE	Never been married (different from "unmarried").
SUBJECT TO	(1) Conditions that have to be met first (i.e., "subject to" the following); (2) Loans that will remain (i.e., "subject to" first trust deed loan).
TC	Tenants in common—type of vesting to hold title in real property.
TD	Trust deed or deed of trust—the document that secures a loan on the property.
TIL	Truth-in-lending disclosure—required document provided by loan officer to disclose the terms and conditions of a loan.
TERM	Time period, usually used to state the length of a loan.
TERMS	The conditions of an agreement, contract, loan.
TITLE	Name of the person or entity who owns or has interest in the property.
TRUST DEED	See "TD."

TRUSTEE	The third party in a trust deed (see above) who will issue the Recon (see above).
TRUSTOR	The person or entity who owes the money on the property; the borrower.
TRUST CERT	Trust certification—document to be completed by trustee that reflects the status of the trust agreement.
UNDERLINING DOCS	The actual recorded documents that describe the items summarized on a preliminary report.
UNDERWRITER	The person at the lender institution who reviews the loan file to see that all of the requirements to approve the loan are submitted before the loan is formally approved (different from loan officer).
UNINSURED DEED	A grant deed or quitclaim deed that was recorded without benefit of title insurance to back it up.
UNMARRIED	Married before but presently not married (different from "single").
VESTING	The manner in which ownership is held by a person or entity, for instance, "joint tenants" or "community property" or "tenants in common."
ZERO DEMAND	A payoff statement from lender to show the amount to be paid is $0.00, or that the loan was paid in full.

About the Author

Juliana Tu has been an Escrow Officer for over 35 years. Her experience comes from handling and managing thousands of different types of escrow/settlement transactions through the years, as well as being a proud survivor of all the crazy roller coaster economic cycles from 1975 through today.

She has been deeply involved in the professional organizations of this industry and has received the following professional designations from the California Escrow Association:

Certified Senior Escrow Officer (CSEO)

Certified Escrow Officer (CEO)

Certified Bulk Sale Specialist (CBSS)

Certified Escrow Instructor (CEI)

Juliana is a proud member of the California Escrow Association (CEA), the American Escrow Association (AEA), and the Escrow Institute of California (EIC). She was appointed to the Department of Corporations Escrow Law Advisory Committee for a two-year period (2012-2014), and she was appointed to the Consumer Financial Protection Bureau's Small Business Review Panel under the Small Business Regulatory Enforcement Act (SBREFA).

Last, but never least, she is the dedicated owner of Viva Escrow! Inc., an independent, minority owned, settlement services company in Los Angeles County, California.

Visit her website at www.vivaescrow.com

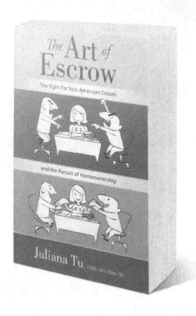

Printed in the USA
CPSIA information can be obtained
at www.ICGtesting.com
JSHW011417160824
R13664500003B/R136645PG68134JSX00040B/23